PENGUIN BOOKS

KID ... n or before
... ill be

Kevin Lewis is thirty-two. H ... th two children
and lives in Surrey.

The Kid
A TRUE STORY

KEVIN LEWIS

PENGUIN BOOKS

PENGUIN BOOKS

Published by the Penguin Group
Penguin Books Ltd, 80 Strand, London WC2R ORL, England
Penguin Group (USA) Inc., 375 Hudson Street, New York, New York 10014, USA
Penguin Books Australia Ltd, 250 Camberwell Road, Camberwell, Victoria 3124, Australia
Penguin Books Canada Ltd, 10 Alcorn Avenue, Toronto, Ontario, Canada M4V 3B2
Penguin Books India (P) Ltd, 11 Community Centre, Panchsheel Park, New Delhi – 110 017, India
Penguin Books (NZ) Ltd, Cnr Rosedale and Airborne Roads, Albany, Auckland, New Zealand
Penguin Books (South Africa) (Pty) Ltd, 24 Sturdee Avenue, Rosebank 2196, South Africa

Penguin Books Ltd, Registered Offices: 80 Strand, London WC2R ORL, England

www.penguin.com

Published by Michael Joseph 2003
Published in Penguin Books 2004
29

Copyright © Kevin Lewis, 2003
All rights reserved

Printed in England by Clays Ltd, St Ives plc

ISBN-13: 978–0–141–01462–3

To my dearest Jackie
My friend, my love, my life
Thank you

Contents

Contents

Acknowledgements

To my literary agent, Barbara Levy, for your support. To my editors, Lindsey Jordan and Louise Moore, and the rest of the team at Michael Joseph – thank you for making a dream come true. A special thank you to Andrew for your help, professionalism and understanding. A rare gift to have all three. Cheers.

Preface

This book was originally written for my wife, Jackie. For many years I've kept my past to myself, ashamed of what happened, desperate to block it out of my memory, until I decided to explain my life to the one person I love more than anything else. I wanted her to understand who I am and what has happened to me in the past.

Once the book was written I decided to publish it in the hope that others would understand what it's like for a child to have no hope; to undergo years of physical and mental torture as well as suffering the constant ache of hunger. I hope I can give a little more insight into why some kids go so badly wrong, so that we can find ways to help them feel less frightened, abandoned and alone in the world.

It was when I was holding my baby son in my arms for the first time that I realized I had to do something about exorcizing the horrors that were locked inside my head. I had to clear them out in order to make sure he had the right start in life. It was a story that could not be allowed to fester in secrecy any longer.

Gazing down at his tiny, sleeping face was like looking at myself when I first arrived in the world. He seemed so vulnerable and helpless and I was desperate to make everything perfect for him, to give him the best start in life that any parent could, to make sure nothing from my past would ever rise up to damage him or make him unhappy. All the memories I'd dampened down and suppressed deep in my subconscious in order to survive began to smoulder and burn, making my eyes water and my chest constrict when I held him in my arms.

My son was our second child, and I had experienced similar fears before. I was so afraid when my daughter was born in 1995 that I would turn out to be a terrible father and would do her some harm. By that time I'd found out some of the secrets that had governed my own childhood and upbringing, and I had no way of knowing if the madness in my parents, which had made my own life a misery for so many years, might also be ticking inside my head, like a time bomb waiting to explode. Everything seemed so perfect in my new life, but it could so easily have gone horribly wrong again just because I didn't know if I would be a good parent. Sometimes I would lie in bed at night with my back to my wife, Jackie, and cry because of what had happened in the past and because I was so frightened the pattern might repeat itself. I still didn't dare to expose the whole story to Jackie or to the outside world. By the time my son came along, three years later, I felt brave enough to face the demons inside my head and to share them with the woman I love and the rest of the world.

I'm not the greatest person for talking about myself, or my feelings. I guess that's obvious since I haven't even been able to tell my own wife about my past, and she's always been kind enough not to ask. But I now believe I owe it to her to explain who I am and to describe some of the places that my early life took me to. I have never been able to tell her face-to-face because I've felt too ashamed, so I decided to put it down on paper instead.

The reason it makes a book, I believe, is because the life I was forced to lead for the first thirty years has been unusual as well as horrifying, and because it shows that it's possible to start with every childhood disadvantage, to travel right to the bottom of the barrel as a young man, so far down that you don't believe life is worth living any more, and still to climb back and achieve a happy and fulfilled life.

I believe readers will be shocked by the way in which a child can still be allowed to slip through the social net in modern Britain, vulnerable to predators and left believing they have no option but to turn to crime. I hope they will be uplifted by the way in which love came to my rescue and perseverance paid off. I'm not proud of everything I did in those early years, but I hope I can show how children like me are left with no other choice if they want to survive. All I wanted was to be given a chance to show what I could do. But so often the outside world is unforgiving of differences it doesn't understand. Children often behave very badly indeed, but there is always a reason, if people will just take the time and trouble to ask the right questions. Perhaps, once you've read my story, you'll have a better idea what questions should be asked and what help should be offered. I hope that you will come away as convinced as I am that small children should never, ever be beaten or abused by the people who are supposed to be their protectors.

I

The Pink Tin House

I was born on 8 September 1970, so this is not a story from the 'bad old days', this all happened at a time when British society was priding itself on becoming enlightened. We had the welfare state and child-protection laws and an army of well-meaning people dedicated to making it a fair world for children born at the bottom of the social heap. But still they couldn't save me from the fate that awaited me in my own home.

On my birth certificate it says we lived in Gypsy Hill, near Crystal Palace in South London, but I only remember living on 'The Horseshoe' – a curve of houses on King Henry's Drive in New Addington, near Croydon in Surrey – so we must have moved there when I was still too young to take in what was happening. It doesn't really matter where we were living because any house that our family occupied would soon have looked the same.

That strip of the South London suburbs was a bleak and culturally desolate area. There was row upon row of twentieth-century social housing provided for those who couldn't afford to live in the city, mixed in with street after street of dreary 'affordable' housing for those who aspired to a more genteel suburban existence. There was no cultural history for the community to feel any pride about, no sense of belonging. In New Addington there was nothing to soothe the eye or the soul. It was just a place where hundreds of thousands of people lived until they could afford to move to somewhere nicer. Many of the families, just like ours, were never going to be going anywhere, trapped in a spiral of poverty, debt and desperation.

King Henry's Drive was a long, busy, depressing road lined by row upon row of tin houses, with the Horseshoe in the middle and tower blocks at the end, and roads either side leading nowhere. The Horseshoe, as the name implies, was a curved side road allowing the houses to be set back from the main road around a large patch of grass. If a private company was building the Horseshoe today it would be called a 'crescent' and would be prettily landscaped with trees, but all we had to look at on the grass was a public phone box and the houses opposite. All the houses around it were built of corrugated tin and were owned by the council. I don't know if the architects who designed them intended these houses to last for more than a few decades, but they are still there today, although some of them have now been improved with new tiles on their roofs and wooden cladding on the outside walls. In the early seventies they were all still just tin boxes for living in, cost-effective places to put families in order to stop them ending up on the street.

Every house in the row was painted a different pastel colour, probably in the hope of lifting the spirits of those who had to live in them and giving the area some sort of character. Ours was pink on the outside, which belied the filth and misery that existed inside those flimsy walls. Behind the house was a garden, which backed on to the car park and playgrounds of Wolsey Junior School.

Some of the neighbours had managed to make their

homes look quite nice, with well-tended front gardens, tubs and hanging baskets, decorative fences and pretty curtains at the windows. Their efforts to add colour and life to their houses merely drew attention to the lack of colour and life all around.

Anything like that would have been completely beyond the abilities or imaginations of Gloria and Dennis, my natural parents. Just existing was almost more than they could manage. Gloria never bothered to change out of her dressing gown unless she was leaving the house to cash her Giro and it never occurred to her that she should even clean her own house, let alone decorate it or improve it in any way. Even today I can't bring myself to call them mother and father. On the rare occasions when I'm talking to one of my brothers or sisters, I always refer to her as 'your mother'. Some wounds are just too deep to ever heal.

Gloria was a giant of a woman, over six feet tall and lean, with all the physical strength of someone constantly supercharged by a powerful bad temper. Dennis was physically strong and silent, whereas Gloria was loud – and she was violent. She never talked in a normal voice, only shouted. She was never calm, always angry. No one liked her, which made her angrier. The neighbours hated the way she was screaming at them one minute and scrounging from them the next; they hated how every other word that came from her mouth was an obscenity. It was a constant, ugly stream of the few most aggressive expletives the English language could supply, fired out by a jet of permanent spite. When she tried to be nice to people outside the family and make them her friends, which wasn't often, she was still too overpowering and they would shrink away from the onslaught of her personality.

Dennis was stocky and much shorter than her. He worked as a British Rail engineer, maintaining the tracks, one of those gangs of men you see sometimes from train windows, out in all weathers in their luminous jackets. He had jet-black hair and was naturally withdrawn. A life spent wandering the rail tracks, never having to deal with the public, must have suited him well. The passion of his life was the music of Elvis Presley. He was a desperately shy man, working every moment he could, sometimes out in the rain and snow or all through the night. But however many hours he put in, he could never make enough money to keep us at anything approaching a decent level. The pressure of it all seemed to be too much for him. The moment he got home from work he would shut himself in the kitchen with his tape machine, just playing Elvis songs over and over again while he stood at the sink, silently drinking. The music must have provided him with an escape from reality, something I later came to appreciate myself, but it certainly didn't give him any joy. It never made him smile or sing along, except when he'd had too much to drink, when he would join in with the most soulful songs. I don't know if the rock and roll even made him want to tap his feet. It was a sticking plaster for his damaged soul rather than a balm. I guess the drinking provided another means of escape, numbing the pain of failure and disappointment for at least a few hours each day.

As far as I know Gloria had never worked, certainly not in my living memory. She was always totally dependent on the welfare state for handouts, but who could blame her when she had so many children to look after? Every Monday she would be queuing up outside the Post Office in the dingy shopping precinct for her Giro with so many others and she would immediately spend it. That Post Office seemed to do more trade than any of the other shops around it. Now they sell lottery tickets as well, so people can buy a few rays of hope with their meagre handouts without even having to leave the premises. Gloria had no budgeting abilities whatsoever. Even if Dennis gave her money during the week, there would still be no food in the house by Friday. She never made any plans or harboured any dreams. She had no hopes of bettering herself or ambitions for us; she lived from one handout to the next without a thought to the future or even a plan to get us safely through to the following Monday and the next Giro.

If the Giro didn't arrive when it should we knew the pressures on us all would increase enormously. She would wait by the window for the postman to come. Very little mail came to our house and if the waiting became too much for her she would send me out, even as young as five, to find the postman in the neighbouring streets and see if he was on his way to the Horseshoe and would be willing to let me run ahead with our mail so she would get it a few minutes earlier so that she could cash it and spend it the moment the shops opened. If the postman didn't have it and I had to return to the house empty-handed I knew I would be in big trouble, and we would have to repeat the whole process when the next post was due.

As children we were always hungry, not able to dull our appetites with drink and cigarettes, as she and Dennis did. From an early age I knew my father liked drinking and smoking and although my mother never drank anything except tea, there was always a smouldering cigarette stuck to her bottom lip.

The house was always in chaos. Anyone glancing in

through an opened door or uncurtained window would have known immediately that we were a family who couldn't cope. In fact they would have known before that from the piles of junk outside the front door. Our clothes were always strewn around the living area on any surface that was free and many that were already cluttered, great limp piles of them would encircle us as we sat on the sofa, or slide to the floor if we bumped against them, where they would remain to be walked across or kicked carelessly into corners. Nothing was ever put away into a cupboard or a drawer; nothing was ever cared for or cherished. The front room always looked like the last hour of a jumble sale, just before the unsaleable items are finally consigned to the tip. In the kitchen there was always washing-up waiting to be done and frying pans would be re-used with the fat of previous meals still clinging to them. Nothing was ever washed up. Everywhere you looked there was filth and disorder.

Gloria ruled the house like the tyrant she was. Some of the rules were completely irrational, but as a child you accept things the way they are. It's only later that you look back and see the gruesome absurdity of it all. We weren't, for instance, allowed to have lights in our bedrooms. Perhaps it was an economy measure, or perhaps they couldn't be bothered to install the bulbs, but looking back now I think it was more likely they wanted to exercise their power over us and let us know they were the masters and we were just mistakes. We may have been great when we were cute little puppies, but as young dogs we needed too much looking after.

The bathroom was on the ground floor with an outside toilet, but we weren't allowed downstairs in the night in case we stole whatever food there might be left in the fridge, so if we needed the toilet we had to use a bucket, which was left out at the top of the stairs. Because it was so dark upstairs we didn't always manage to hit the bucket, and the puddles were allowed to soak into the bare boards, creating a tacky patina of stains. Sometimes the smaller children didn't even make a pretence of using the bucket, they just peed wherever they felt like it. The whole house stank of urine.

There was no paper on any of the walls, or if there was it was hanging off in strips. If anything was broken or stained it stayed that way. The bedrooms were just bare, dingy cells where we tried to hide from Gloria's tempers. The walls were drawn on and sometimes smeared with human excrement, where small children had had accidents and no one had bothered to clear it up. The floors upstairs and downstairs were always sticky with grime and in the few areas where there were remnants of carpet, they were black with filth and ragged with years of wear and neglect. It was like living in a derelict house, one that was just waiting for the demolition crew to arrive or for homeless youths to move in and squat. But it wasn't derelict, it was our family home.

Electricity and gas were always a problem. We had to have meters installed because Gloria and Dennis never paid the bills, and even then they were always robbing the fifty pence pieces, breaking in and then wedging the fronts open. We'd sometimes go for days with no power at all because they'd broken the equipment or had run out of money and we'd have to wait till the following Monday for the same ritual of waiting for the postman to arrive. Since we never had any money, we always owed people. Whenever the gas, electricity or rent people came knocking we were told to hide, diving for cover behind the sofa, or simply pulling a pile of clothes over us, hoping that if they peered through the windows they'd just see a scene of deserted chaos. If that failed, and they managed to get into the house, there would always be a shouting match with accusations flying back and forth and Gloria boiling with righteous indignation at the unfairness of life.

Occasionally my older brother Wayne and I would pluck up the courage to steal from the fridge while our parents were preoccupied somewhere else in the house, driven on by the ache of hunger that constantly gnawed at our insides. We trained ourselves to creep downstairs in the dead of night, knowing what floorboards to avoid treading on in order not to be heard. There was never much to choose from, but anything we found we would cram into our mouths, swallowing it as quickly as possible in case we were caught and forced to spit it out. We'd wolf down raw sausages if that was all there was, or raw potatoes. Dennis had a liking for veal and ham pies and if he left one overnight in the fridge we'd try to get it, willing to brave the consequences in order to lessen the pain of hunger.

Like many small boys I used to wet the bed almost every night and I would call out to my mother, scared of telling her but not knowing what else to do. I soon learned not to tell Gloria because then she would smack me on my wet skin, which made the blows sting even more, and she would push me downstairs and force me to sleep in the bath with just a dirty towel as a blanket to teach me a lesson.

'You dirty, fucking cunt!' she'd scream into my sleep-fuddled ear in the early hours of the morning, furious at being woken up from her own exhausted slumbers, pushing and pinching and slapping at any part of me I didn't manage to get out of her reach.

I'd do as she told me as quickly as possible, lying in the cold, hard bath until she'd gone back upstairs, and then I'd creep out on to the bathroom floor, trying to find another towel to lie on as it was warmer than the cold metal of the bath. Desperate not to fall too deeply asleep, in case I didn't hear her coming back downstairs in the morning, I'd then doze fitfully for the rest of the night. The moment I heard her stirring upstairs I'd climb back into the bathtub and feign deep sleep. I soon learnt not to wake her when I had accidents if I could help it. I discovered that if I lay long enough on the wet patch the heat from my body would dry it. She would never notice the stain because she never changed the beds. The smell of dirt and urine permeated us as well as our surroundings, travelling with us to school the next day in our clothes and hair and on our skins.

My nights were often as frightening as the days, haunted by nightmares. I would sometimes wake up in the dark room and cry out for my mother without thinking, but as soon as I heard her stamping towards the room I would instantly regret it, curling up into a ball, pulling the covers over my head to counteract the inevitable blows that would rain down. I had to learn as early as possible to curb my natural childish instincts to turn to my mother when I was frightened or unhappy. I had to learn to hold the fear and misery inside, to cope with them myself, because if I annoyed her in any way with my problems I would simply make everything worse.

'You make another fucking sound, you fucking cunt,' she would scream at the top of her voice as I tried to hug her and tell her what had frightened me, 'you'll get the shit kicked out of you, and you'll be sleeping in the bath.'

Nightmares were punishable in exactly the same way as

bed-wetting. She would drag me down the stairs by my hair to the bathroom. I learnt to cling on to her hands when she had hold of my hair, to take off some of the weight and lessen the pain. There are always tricks you can employ, usually instinctively, to increase the chances of survival in any situation. The more I screamed and pleaded for mercy the more furious she would become, so I learnt not to cry, to keep as quiet as possible. I reasoned that if I took the punishment in silence it would all be over quicker, but sometimes my silent acceptance of the punishment simply fuelled her fury. I would stand there flinching, my lip trembling and silent tears running down my face. She would see it as some sort of dumb insolence and keep attacking me until I was unable to stop myself from crying out in pain. I think she needed to hear the screams of pain to prove she was in control.

Her anger always and immediately erupted into violence; sometimes she'd lash out at us with her hands and feet, sometimes she'd grab a stick or a belt or anything else that came to hand in order to make the beatings more effective. If she hit me with her hand, the blow was so hard there would be a raised imprint of the palm and big fingers left on my skin for hours afterwards. In some of the worst furies she would be biting and scratching us in the sort of frenzy you might associate with a wild dog. The best way of defending myself was to curl up into a ball, guarding my face and vital organs. I was too young to defend myself, just pleading for mercy, 'Sorry, Mummy! Sorry, Mummy! Please no, Mum! Please no, Mum!' and on and on.

One night – I must have been no more than six years old – I woke from a deep sleep with an unfamiliar feeling. Someone was holding me, but it wasn't the usual sort of holding. I wasn't being restrained, or pulled painfully in some direction I didn't want to go. There didn't seem to be any anger involved or shouting. I was confused in my half-awake state, knowing that I felt comfortable and protected, but not knowing why. As I came round I realized the house was full of unusual activity. The arms I was cradled in were unfamiliar. They were a man's arms and although he was taking care not to alarm me he was hurrying. There was a sense of urgency and I could hear voices and the noise of running engines outside the house as we made our way downstairs. As we came into the illuminated night I saw that the man who was holding me was wearing a helmet and uniform, and I realized he was a fireman. I didn't feel frightened because he seemed so calm as he took me out into the street. I didn't appear to be in any danger.

There was a smell of smoke and a lot of noise coming from the fire engines that were parked by the curb, putting out the fire that had broken out in the tin house next door. I was sad when he put me down to watch the goings-on with the others. I'll never forget the feeling of being carried for those few moments by that fireman; I'd never experienced anything so gentle or caring before.

My brother, Wayne, was just a year older than me and, below us, were Sharon and Julie. Robert and Brenda came along later. Gloria always preferred Wayne to me, and Sharon and Julie were much quieter and less likely to annoy her. So it was me she hated with the greatest vehemence, until Robert arrived to share my role as her scapegoat. Brenda, the baby of the family, would always be her other favourite, along with Wayne. It was a situation we all understood and accepted. It was just the way things were.

Gloria didn't confine herself to physical bullying. As she punched and kicked, scratched and slapped me, pulling my hair and sometimes even biting me, she would also rain down abuse, telling me I was 'pathetic', that I was 'gay'. 'Kevin is a gay little bastard,' she would repeat over and over again. All the time she was telling me how useless I was, her face would be an inch away from mine, her teeth gritted in fury and the four-letter words punching into me. All the frustrations and hardships that were constantly building up inside her own head would spew out over me every time I came near her, every hour of every day. The aggression never relented. Her dislike for me was so intense that even when she was in a good mood she couldn't bring herself to speak kindly to me or to hug me or kiss me. I never heard a single word of praise or kindness pass her lips. Sometimes she'd become so incensed with me her false teeth would jump loose as she shouted. Whenever that happened I could never resist laughing, which would add even more fuel to her rage. To me this was normal life.

The moment Dennis came back into the house from work she would be screaming out lists of my misdemeanours. 'Your fucking son's done this, and that . . .' It was the same every single day. Her endless tirade would drive him straight through to the kitchen as she pelted him with hysterical complaints and abuse until he could get his tape machine going and a bottle open, to drown her voice out with Elvis and beer.

I don't remember what my crimes were in those early days. I was a lively, boisterous boy, so they could have been anything from breaking a cup to slamming a door or eating something that was forbidden, giving her a bad look or being overexcited because I was going outside to play.

Sometimes it was nothing at all. It didn't matter what I did or didn't do, the reaction would always be the same.

There were social workers coming to the house now and then, but they never stayed for long, and if any of my marks or bruises were visible they could always be explained away with some invented accident or other. 'He fell over in the garden!' she'd say and they'd look out at the three-foot-high grass with the debris poking out of it and decide they had no reason to doubt her story. The moment they walked through the door she would be pouring out her tales of hardship and streams of bile against anyone who had upset her. You could see the panic in their eyes as they tried to get away from her barrage of complaints and grievances about us, about Dennis, about the neighbours, the council and anyone else who had touched her life in the previous few days or weeks. They couldn't wait to get back out of the house into the fresh air, so they didn't prolong their visits unnecessarily by talking to me or asking me how I was.

They could see she and I hated each other, but they had no proof that she was hitting me. If they did ask me how I'd come by a particular cut or bruise, I'd lie for her, because if I didn't I knew I'd be beaten to even more of a pulp the moment they were out of the door. She would be standing there, towering over me as the social worker knelt down to talk to me. I never knew why they came to us or what they did, but whenever they were there Gloria was on her best behaviour, like a child being good for sweets.

There was no escape for me. I couldn't outrun her. I couldn't hide from her. I had no choice but to continue to live in fear and stay silent about it.

Once Dennis was home and in the kitchen she still

wouldn't allow him to listen to his music in peace. She'd be determined to involve him in the disciplining of his children. No one in the family ever spoke quietly. There were never any reasonable conversations. Everyone would be screaming at once and he would inevitably be dragged into the affray, his patience stretched as tightly as hers by the endless noise and foul language. Eventually, particularly once he'd got a few drinks inside him, he'd start hitting out as well. Because she wouldn't let up, going on and on about everything that was wrong in her life, everything that was wrong with him and with me, he would be unable to withstand the pressure any longer. After a long hard day, or night, of physical labour he would snap and they would start to argue. They would hit each other and, if we were within reach, they would both hit out at us as well.

Once tempers were lost we were all in real danger of being seriously hurt by both of them. Both lost all sense of judgement when their anger bubbled over. When Wayne back-chatted him one time, Dennis threw a knife at him. Wayne can't have been more than six or seven. We were all there in the room; Gloria, me and Dennis shouting, the girls watching in nervous silence. He could have thrown anything in his fury; it just happened to be a knife that came into his hand at the moment his temper snapped and he didn't have the control to stop himself. The blade dug into Wayne's leg and the blood immediately started to flow. A loud panic mixed with anger filled the house as they tried to work out what they should be doing and calm themselves enough to act responsibly. When they finally realized they couldn't treat the wound adequately themselves, they were forced to take Wayne down to the hospital to be stitched up. They must have been nervous that they'd be asked awkward questions. When the harassed doctor asked what had happened they told him it had been an accident and he accepted the explanation. It continually amazed me how people in positions to rescue us were always happy to believe whatever they were told by adults. It must have been obvious from the state we were in that things were out of control, but all the people we came into contact with were always willing to take whatever explanation Gloria or Dennis came up with. Maybe it was pressures of time or workload that made them so anxious to move on to the next problem, or maybe they didn't want to interfere, or maybe we were just too scary a prospect for most normal people to be able to face.

Dennis was a very strong man physically. When he was hitting me he would lift me up by my wrist, leaving my other hand free to frantically try to block the blows as I squirmed and wriggled in his grip, but it was impossible and my efforts at self-protection and my refusal to remain a stationary target only made him angrier. Wayne, Julie and Sharon would become afraid when he lost his temper with me, screaming at him to stop hitting me, but their noise would only annoy him more, like a dazed, confused bull being taunted in a bullring. Once he'd smacked me with all his strength he would toss me aside like a piece of dirty laundry. But his eruptions would pass, unlike Gloria's, and he would never scream abuse into my face or tell me what a useless little bastard I was. I got the impression he liked me, that I was his favourite, but he just couldn't handle the strain of the constant noise and the screaming and the anger. He just wanted to be left alone with his beer and his music.

The constant noise must have been like a torture for him, gradually driving him further and further inside himself. He became quieter and more withdrawn with every passing year. There were moments when we got glimpses of the sort of father he might have been if he hadn't been under too much pressure from us all. Once, when Wayne and I were squabbling about something, he gave us both boxing gloves and told us to fight properly if we were going to, believing that the only way to sort anything out was through violence and abuse. Sometimes, if I'd taken a real bashing from Gloria, I'd walk past him and he would put his hand on my shoulder, but he never said anything. When that happened I thought that everything would be all right, but it never was. I thought that he would protect me and look after me, but he never did.

As the years went by his drinking became worse. He moved from beer to gin, coming home every night with half bottles tucked into his pocket and staying in the kitchen until the small hours just drinking and listening to the music. None of us went in there; we knew he wanted to be left alone. The harder he drank the angrier and more depressed he became, withdrawing further into himself.

There was nothing in the house except anger and unhappiness, nightmares and rows, beatings and abuse. There were no saving moments of laughter or forgiveness, no kind words or encouragement for any of us. Life under those circumstances beats down a child's self-esteem and gives them no hope for the future. There is only endurance, never enjoyment. If something or someone else doesn't come along to save them, the children of such families have no hope of escape and merely repeat the pattern set by their parents.

2

The Tramps

If home life was a continuous nightmare, there was no escape for us when we got to school either. The other children called us 'the tramps' and excluded us totally. It was obvious we were different to them, and everyone in the area knew of Gloria so we were branded with her reputation as well. I'm sure the parents of other children were warning them to stay away from us. No one would have wanted their children to become involved with us. If I'd been one of those parents, I suspect I would have been discouraging my children from having anything to do with us.

We were enrolled at Wolsey Junior, the school that lay just behind our house, so the other kids could see the way we lived with their own eyes. Our garden only had chicken wire around it, so we couldn't hide the squalor from anyone passing by. Just the other side of the wire the parents would gather twice a day to drop off and pick up their kids. They would be standing in groups talking, as parents do, and right beside them was the glaring evidence of how far out of control our home life was. I burned with shame when I saw them looking through the wire at the bombsite inside and heard them lowering their voices to exchange anecdotes about us. I became certain that every pair of eyes that ever came to the school was irresistibly drawn to the horrors of our back garden.

The parents might have lowered their voices when they talked about us, but kids don't bother about being polite or sparing people's feelings. They're just looking for reasons to put other people down before someone puts them down, and my parents provided plenty of those, from the way we dressed to the way we smelt, from the squalor of the house to the constant shouting.

Sometimes Gloria would strip wash us in the kitchen sink in front of the window, so anyone going to or from the school could see us, naked and humiliated, being washed down in the kitchen amongst the filthy plates and pans. Sunday night was bath night. If we were out playing on the grass of the Horseshoe when she was ready to start the ritual, we'd hear her bellowing for us to come in, her ugly voice drowning out every other sound. We didn't dare to loiter once she had called, knowing we would receive a beating once she got us if we made her wait.

If I wasn't the first in line for the bath I would have to sit and listen to the inconsolable screams of the others, staring at the television, trying to concentrate on *Playaway*, or some other programme, to dull the noise, completely silent, knowing what was coming as I waited my turn. They were genuine screams of fear and pain.

Once she had hold of us she'd scrub us painfully hard and dig out our ears with a hairpin – you never knew how deep she'd push that pin in and I always feared she would break through my eardrum and make me deaf. If I tried to struggle she'd pin my arms to my sides with a towel and finish the job by force. Once I'd given up the fight and was restrained, I lay still and silent because if I'd moved my head the hairpin would have gone deeper and the damage and pain would have been worse.

The agonizing discipline of those ritual cleansings still clings to me and I find I have to clean my ears out every day, even when I know they don't need it, although I now use cotton buds not pieces of metal. We didn't have any shampoo or decent soap so the baths barely scraped the surface of our dirt, and we then climbed back into stinking clothes and bedding, so our distinctive family smell remained undiminished.

Sometimes the other kids would set up a chant in the playground when we arrived: 'Tramp! Tramp! Tramp!', or any other choice phrase they decided to bellow at us. There was nothing we could do to stop them. We had to brazen it out. There was nowhere to run to and we couldn't fight all of them. There was nothing we could do to improve our appearance; we were who we were and we couldn't do anything to change it. There was nothing we could do about the dirt or the smell because we didn't know how to fumigate the house or launder the sheets and clothes any more than Gloria did. None of us owned a toothbrush or knew what toothpaste was, or even used soap regularly. The stigma of an undignified poverty clung to us as stubbornly as the smells and the other children didn't intend to let us forget our place.

There is no shame in not having money, but even at the poorest levels of society there are still social grades. There are those who work honestly to give their children the best upbringing they can within their limited means, lavishing them with love and keeping them clean, helping them with their schoolwork in the hope they might later be able to escape the poverty trap, even if their parents can't. These people have self-respect and they know there is a better life to be striven for. Then there are the families who just don't care, who seem to wallow in their own squalor, and who've given up all hope of ever improving their lot in life. The children of poor families have no difficulty in distinguishing between the two types. No prizes for guessing where the Lewis family fell in this hierarchy of poverty.

We lived in social isolation. No other children ever invited us back to their homes to play and we were too frightened to invite them back to our house because of what they would have seen. The shame of opening the door to anyone else would have been too much to bear. How can you invite a classmate to your bedroom when you know it stinks of urine because there is an unemptied bucket of the stuff at the top of the stairs, and when there isn't even a light bulb so they could see to play? I suspect their parents wouldn't have let them come anyway.

We never went to anyone's birthday parties. It always puzzled me that I knew these parties went on because I would hear the others talking about them in the playground the day after, but I never actually saw them happening. They were something that existed outside my little world. In my imagination they became something wonderful, like everything else that I felt excluded from. I longed to be someone else, someone who was invited to parties, someone who was popular and had friends and wasn't different. The other parents wouldn't encourage their children to be kind to us. They didn't want to become involved with the aggressive Gloria and her miserable, silent husband. Looking back now, I really don't blame them. They were just protecting their children. But it meant there was nowhere we could turn where we would get any respite from the beating and bullying at home and the taunting of the playground. We were outsiders in every area of our lives.

Not only did we not get invited to other children's birthday parties, we didn't have any of our own either. Gloria would never have been able to organize anything like that. Where would she have got the money? How would she have persuaded anyone else to set foot inside our house? Where would she have put guests amongst the dirty clothes and other detritus of our lives? How would she have known, any more than I did, what a party involved? She didn't know any games. She couldn't cook. Where would she have got a cake from? None of this was part of Gloria's world. Dennis wouldn't have been any better. How could a man too shy to talk to his own family cope with playing games with other people's children? The whole idea would have been impossible.

I have no memory of ever receiving any birthday presents at all. Wayne and the girls used to get something from Gloria, but whenever it was my turn there was always a problem with the Giro 'not clearing'.

'I'll get you something next week,' she might promise if she felt the slightest twinge of guilt when I came hurrying downstairs on my birthday morning. 'When I get the money.' But she never did.

Despite the evidence which built, year upon year, I always lived in hope that things would change and that my next birthday would become a celebration, a day when I would be special for at least a few hours. Children are optimistic creatures at heart. It takes a lot to convince them that the world is really against them and that things will not improve one day. The day before my seventh birthday I was brimming with ideas of what I was going to receive the next day. As Wayne and I came downstairs to get ready for school I was burbling away to him about everything I was expecting to get.

Gloria must have heard me; I was not a quiet child, used to shouting to make myself heard over everyone else. Perhaps she felt I was criticizing her by listing the things she'd never have thought of getting me and wouldn't have had the money for anyway. Perhaps she felt momentarily guilty, or angry at my presumption. Whatever the reason, she caught me by surprise, stamping across the hall and grabbing me by the back of my jumper before I had time to wriggle past her. She hauled me up off my feet, the neck of the jumper cutting into my throat. I couldn't breathe. As I flailed around in the air, desperately struggling to get some breath into my lungs, she yanked my trousers down with her free hand and started laying into me with my own belt.

I tried to put one hand behind me to intercept the blows, while I struggled to pull my collar away from my windpipe with the other hand. My feeble attempts at defending myself seemed to stoke up her fury. She hurled me to the floor and the moment I was able to fill my lungs I started to scream with pain and shock. All my determination not to cry in front of her again had deserted me. My screams seemed to make her even angrier. She came after me again before I could get away, grabbing my hair and dragging me into the lounge, my trousers and pants still down round my knees, my buttocks and back burning from the blows.

As I struggled to get free she picked me up as if I was a pile of old clothes and chucked me across the width of the room. I remember those few seconds of hanging in the air, like I could fly, before I crashed down on to the window ledge, hitting my head on the corner. It was like an explosion going off inside my brain.

I stopped screaming, feeling dazed and disoriented,

unsure exactly what had happened to me. I don't know if I passed out. There was a splitting pain in my head and I could feel the warm wetness of blood on my face. I put my hands up to touch it and they turned red in front of my eyes. Gloria had stopped shouting too and I could hear her panting in the silence that had fallen over the house. After a few seconds Wayne recovered from the shock and started yelling and the girls were crying again. I wasn't making any sound, just shaking uncontrollably and staring at the blood, trying to work out what I should do, wanting someone to take me in their arms and sort me out.

She turned and stamped out of the room, returning a few moments later with a dirty flannel from the bathroom, which she threw down to me.

'Clean yourself up and fuck off to school!' she snarled.

I went to the bathroom and tried to mop up the mess. My face was a shocking sight and the water just seemed to spread the blood around. It was still coming out and I held the flannel tightly to it to stop the flow. I was anxious to get out of the house without making her any angrier. My legs were wobbling as I made my way to the door. Wayne opened it for me and we stepped out into the fresh air, both shaking and shocked. We turned left past the next-door house and then turned left into the alleyway that ran between the houses that led to the school entrance. It was about a hundred yards long, with high fences and hedges on either side, so no one could see us. Once we were out of sight of the window I felt Wayne taking hold of my hand as we walked together without saying a word. This tiny gesture of kindness made me want to cry, but I held on. I didn't want anyone to see tears when we reached the playground. As soon as we stumbled out of the dark alley into the school grounds we let go of each other and I took a deep breath, determined to keep going and not faint.

I must have been conspicuous amongst the other children, even by my standards, because one of the teachers came straight over to me. She gently turned my face with her fingers and looked at the side of my head.

'I think we should get that looked at by the nurse,' she said, leading me away from the others. Wayne watched me go, but didn't say anything. I followed her, just wanting someone to take control and make everything better.

As I sat in the nurse's room on my own, waiting for something to happen, I could hear school life going on outside the door. Inside the room it smelled clean and safe, an antiseptic place where people were comforted and made well. In the cruel world outside bells rang in a familiar fashion, but didn't seem to be anything to do with me. For a few moments I had been lifted out of my troubled life and allowed to rest. There were the sounds of running feet and voices shouting and laughing. I'd had trouble sitting down when we first came in because of a pain in my lower back and I saw the teacher looking at me in a curious fashion before she went off to find the nurse. For a short time I'd been absolved of the responsibility of being part of the school day. It was like a respite; time to gather my thoughts and my strength. I must have been in a fair amount of shock, everything had happened so fast. Just a few minutes earlier I'd been coming downstairs, chattering about my approaching birthday, and now I was hurting all over and receiving special attention. I must admit that the attention felt good, even with the attached pain. I wanted to stay in that safe room for as long as possible.

Other grown-ups started coming into the room, looking

at me. I can't remember who they were or if I recognized them. Someone asked me to lift up my shirt at the back and pull down the waistband of my trousers. I knew I hadn't said anything to give Gloria away. It wasn't going to be my fault if they'd seen I couldn't move properly. I hadn't betrayed her trust. They were very matter-of-fact about it all, but I could tell they were taking things seriously. I was worried they might be going to say something to Gloria. If they did that I'd be in for an even worse beating when she next got me on my own in the house. The only option I could see was to run away at the end of the school day. I began to lay plans for where I would go to and how I would survive the night. There were some woods a mile or two away, surrounding a golf course. If I could get myself there I could live in the woods like I'd seen children doing in programmes on the telly. I didn't think Gloria or Dennis would bother to come looking for me, and I doubted if they would want to tell the authorities that I'd disappeared. I could stay there until it was time to come back to school.

The nurse carefully patched up my head and cleaned the rest of the caked blood away. She was so kind and gentle and caring, so different to Gloria whose hands never touched me unless it was to slap or pinch or punch. I began to feel better. The shaking had stopped and I thought I could manage to go into school with the others. The nurse said she'd take me to the dining room to get a drink. As I came out of her room I had to walk past the queue of children waiting to go into assembly. Every pair of eyes turned to look at me; not just the children but the teachers as well. No one said anything. They just stared as I walked through the gauntlet of eyes. I stared back, not able to understand what was so fascinating about a bit of sticking plaster on a head wound. It'd been a bad morning, but not particularly out of the ordinary as far as I was concerned. Why were they all so transfixed?

The school day went on as usual, but my fear of going home increased as the time passed and I continued to refine my plans for running away. It was a scary prospect, but not as scary as the thought of Gloria waiting for me behind the front door. At the end of lessons, however, the decision was taken out of my hands. I was told to wait because I wasn't going to be going home. My first reaction was relief at the thought that I wasn't going to have to run away and live in the woods with all their strange noises.

'We're going to take you somewhere safe for a little while,' a teacher told me.

I was now scared again, this time of the unknown. If life was bad at home and at school, and even in my nightmares, it might be even worse in whatever place they were planning to take me. I had no reason to believe that there was anywhere where I would actually be happy.

'Can't I go home?' I wanted to know. It felt like I was being punished, but I didn't understand what I'd done wrong. Despite everything that I went through at Gloria's hands, it was still my home, still the place that was most familiar to me, and the place where Wayne and my sisters would be. I didn't know where they were going to be taking me and the unknown is even more frightening than the known, especially when you're not quite seven and all your experience tells you that the world is an unkind place.

They reassured me and a woman I didn't know led me outside to a waiting car. I'd never been in a car before. It was exciting climbing in through the opened door. The interior smelt clean and different from anything I'd experienced before. When the door slammed shut I was cocooned into a new world, a means of escape from the tiny life I was used to, which consisted of my house and school. They were all I'd experienced until that moment and now I was being taken into the unknown with no preparation. As the car set off I almost immediately felt queasy from the unfamiliar movement.

Despite the excitement of the car journey and the anticipation of an adventure, I still felt a strong urge to run back to my dark, dreary little bedroom and hide my head under the musty, familiar smelling sheets. I missed Wayne, Sharon and Julie. I had no idea what to expect next. It was 1977 when I was first taken into care.

3

The Bear Under the Bed

I was taken to an emergency children's home in Croydon. Because it was going to be my birthday the next day, someone gave me a little koala bear and a Womble. I could hardly believe they were for me. I clung to them as if my life depended on it.

By the time we reached the home, which stood opposite Selsdon Station, it was dark. I was given a bath, some clean clothes, a fresh white bandage for my head and something to eat. There was a nasty looking bruise around the cut, making it look more serious than it probably was. All evening I held on tightly to my new friends, the koala and the Womble, watching wide-eyed as the other children and the staff went about what must have been their normal evening routines.

I was nervous because I was in unfamiliar surroundings, but it was a different nervousness to the one I felt at home. It was more exciting, as if I was on the brink of a great adventure. I was also on my guard, expecting someone to be nasty to me at any moment. Experience had taught me that sooner or later I always got hit or shouted at by someone, no matter how careful I was to stay out of the way. I waited to see what would happen.

The evening passed without anyone doing or saying anything unpleasant and I felt encouraged. When I was taken up to bed I was struck by how different the bedclothes and mattress smelled to the one at home. It was a clean smell that I'd never experienced before, more like the nurse's room at school than any of the bedrooms in our house. There was a bright light, so I was able to see what I was doing as I got into clean pyjamas, brushed my teeth as they showed me and climbed into bed. I lay between the stiff, freshly laundered white sheets and breathed deeply, sucking in the aroma, wanting to remember it for ever. It was a beautiful feeling. I must have fallen asleep very quickly, exhausted by a day that had been so strange and so draining, both physically and emotionally. I hugged the koala and Womble tightly to me, my two new best friends.

The next morning I met more of the staff and other children, all of whom looked older than me, and they all sang 'happy birthday' to me over breakfast. It was a nice feeling to be the centre of such pleasant attention, but disconcerting; I didn't know how I was supposed to react. As soon as the meal was over I made my way back up to my little bedroom to find the koala and Womble. They weren't in the bed where I'd left them, carefully tucked up. I lifted the sheets and rummaged around for them, but the bed was empty. Feeling a twinge of panic, I looked all round the room and knelt down to peer under the bed. My two new friends lay on the floor in the darkest corner, their stuffing hanging out of their slashed stomachs, their severed limbs hanging loose. They'd been ripped beyond hope; there was nothing that could be done to repair them. I think someone on the staff gave me something to replace them, but it didn't feel the same because the first two friends I had ever had had been cruelly murdered. Now I knew that even if someone did give me something, someone else would always take it away or destroy it. I didn't want to get attached to anything else, only to lose it the next day.

When I found them I sat on the floor and cried, unable to stop the tears that I'd been holding back for so many hours. It seemed that there was nowhere I could go that would be safe. I wished I was back home with Wayne and the others, at least then I would know what was going to happen next. Now I was facing an invisible and unknown enemy.

As the days passed my enemies became all too visible. Having waited to see what sort of victim I was likely to be, they pounced mercilessly. Being so young, and so naïve, having had no experience outside my own limited family circle, I was a sitting target for the other, bigger children, many of whom needed no excuse to pick on someone younger and more gullible than themselves. Gloria had taught me that it was futile to stand up to bullies because if I ever stood up to her I'd just be beaten all the harder. The other children soon realized that I was an easy victim, someone who was used to taking whatever punishment they cared to dole out without fighting back. I guess these were children who had suffered at the hands of others themselves and were all too keen to pass their suffering on down the line. I was the one at the end of the line.

Those few memories are fairly sharp, although they may be tinged with inaccuracy due to the fact that I was so young and so many years have passed, but around them has settled a fog of half-remembered scenes and faces that populated the following months. I wasn't taken back home. I remained in a no man's land of different children's homes, schools and short-term foster parents, all with their different smells and sounds; all bringing on different memories of anxiety and unhappiness. Sometimes, even now, a whiff of a particular institutional floor polish or disinfectant will bring back a sharp stab of remembered fear and trepidation. Through the fog I can make out a memory of going to a juvenile court. It must have been something to do with the authorities wanting to gain an emergency custodial ruling. Gloria and Dennis were both there. It seemed strange to see them outside the setting of the home; Gloria dressed to face the outside world instead of in her usual grubby dressing gown. It was puzzling to see her but not frightening. She always behaved well towards me when there were other people around. I was physically safer now, even if I didn't feel emotionally secure.

Each time I went to a new foster family I arrived with the knowledge that I would soon be moved on, so I held a bit of myself back every time. I didn't want to allow myself to feel too at home if I was going to have to say goodbye a few weeks later. I knew that all these people were being paid to have me, that I wasn't really part of their families, just a boarder. I knew that none of them actually wanted me for myself. None of their faces has remained clear in my memory.

I learnt a lot about how other families worked, and I was an eager pupil, watching everything, always wary in case I did or said the wrong thing and turned them against me. I was desperate to please and sometimes my eagerness irritated people. One set of foster parents had a boy and girl of their own, both older than me, so the parents can't have been that young. What astonished me about this couple was that they kept kissing each other. They didn't seem able to keep their hands off one another. I'd never seen Gloria and Dennis show each other the slightest flicker of affection, either physical or emotional. I couldn't work out what these two were up to. They took me to visit one of their mums and as we went up to her flat in the lift they went into a clinch, with me staring up at them, open-mouthed. That, I decided, must be what love looked like.

I don't suppose I was an easy child for other people to take into their families. Having been a virtual prisoner in a few rooms for so long the scent of freedom was very heady for me. I was a boisterous little boy and I would have considered it normal to behave with my foster families as I did at home. There was never any love or affection shown between any of us, it was all spite and violence, and I dare-say some of the families found me too aggressive towards their children as I tried to adjust to the outside world. I tried to behave as I thought they wanted, but sometimes it just didn't come out right. Despite all this, it was still a hundred times better than being at home with Gloria.

My new nomadic life went on for a year, while everyone tried to make up their minds what to do with me. It's my impression that had I been younger someone would have adopted me, but an energetic seven-year-old with a difficult family in the background is a lot for anyone to want to take on permanently. After a year everything changed again. It was now 1978.

4

The Birthday Party

The day before my eighth birthday I was told I was going to be moved again, to another home called Yarborough Children's Home. It was in East Grinstead, a genteel, market town in East Sussex. I was nervous about moving back into an institution from the foster home I was in, remembering how unhappy I'd been at the first place in Croydon. I would rather have stayed in family homes, even if I still had to move around every few months.

'We've had to work hard to get you into Yarborough,' the social worker told me. 'It's a very nice place and they don't often have vacancies. You're a lucky boy.' I decided to reserve my judgement until I'd seen what lay in store.

After we'd driven for a while towards East Grinstead the woman asked if I was hungry. I said I was and she pulled off the road into a car park beside a country bakery and café, which had signs advertising its homemade bread, pies and cakes. We went inside and the warm smell of baking was almost overwhelming. I'd never been inside a place with such delicious smells. There were trays on display filled with cakes, pastries, buns, pies and loaves of bread. The woman asked me which one I'd like and I pointed to one, having no idea what any of them were as I couldn't read the labels. It didn't matter what it was, just the texture of freshly baked pastry was more than enough to excite my taste buds. We returned to the car and I ate my treat greedily as we drove on.

As we drove into East Grinstead I could already see that it was unlike the areas I was used to. Although we were in an area which I guess you would call suburban, the atmosphere was very different. The houses, many of them substantial Edwardian and Victorian red-brick villas, were set in large gardens and surrounded by mature trees which gave them privacy. The streets were quiet and well maintained. There was a feeling of space, solidity and greenness. I didn't think that anyone like Gloria lived near here.

We eventually drew up outside one of these red-brick buildings, although this one was a little larger than the others. It didn't look like a family home, but it didn't exactly look like an institution either. On one side an unmade road full of potholes disappeared past playing fields and trees, on the other stood the smart gates of a small private school.

The social worker told me we had reached our destination and we climbed out of the car. She led me through the gates and up to the house. My first impression was of big white double doors in a glazed wooden porch, which we stood in while we waited for someone to answer the bell. When the doors eventually swung open a man who looked, to me, like a giant, towered over us. I stepped back in shock. I stared up at him in awe and he looked me straight in the eye, taking no notice of the grown-up accompanying me. He then crouched down to my level and shook my hand firmly.

'You must be Kevin,' he said. I nodded. 'Will you call me Uncle David?'

I nodded again, dumbstruck. He gave me a wink, pulled himself up once more to his full height, picked my bag up in one hand and held out his other hand for me to take. I gripped it as tightly as I could, terrified at what new experiences I was about to encounter, and he led me into my new home.

The house was fairly quiet, all the children still being at school, and he took me around, introducing me to the staff and showing me the big rooms filled with games and toys. I felt overawed and didn't say much. As the afternoon wore on the children came back from school and I was introduced to them. It wasn't a big home, no more than twenty or so children, but it meant a lot of new faces to take in all at once. I needn't have worried. The others swept me up and took me off. We immediately started running around, laughing and playing while the grown-ups prepared tea. For the first time in my life I felt I'd reached a safe place and the fears I'd come to think of as normal simply drained away. The social worker had been right. This was a very nice place indeed and I was a very lucky boy.

Behind the house was a garden with climbing frames that seemed enormous to me. There was a games room with a billiards table and the whole place felt like one large home rather than an institution. High fences and walls surrounded the premises and we could often hear the happy sounds of the little children laughing and screaming as they ran around the school playground next door.

'How long will I be here?' I asked Uncle David that evening, dreading the answer, never wanting to leave such a wonderful place.

'There are no plans to move you anywhere else, Kevin,' he said. 'We want to keep you here, if you'd like to stay.'

'Yes, please,' I replied, happily.

Although I hadn't told anyone, they obviously knew from

my case notes that it was my birthday the next day. I hadn't bothered to mention it to the other children, as I still didn't think it meant anything. My birthdays had never worked out very well in the past, so I thought it best not to get my hopes up. My optimism on that front had finally run out. That night I was sleeping in the same room as two brothers, Mark and Chris Wallace, who had already become my friends. Mark, who was the same age as me, woke me up in the morning.

'Kevin,' he said, shaking me, 'Kevin, it's your birthday. Come on, we've got to go downstairs.' It seemed like a ritual they'd performed many times before.

Immediately awake, I went down with them to find the breakfast table covered in presents and cards. I'd never seen so many, and they were actually properly gift-wrapped, with my name written on them. All the cards and labels had signatures of who had given them, but I couldn't make them out because I still hadn't learnt to read. If anyone in my family had ever received a present the only wrapping was likely to be the carrier bag it had come from the shop in.

I couldn't stop opening the presents, spreading the brightly coloured paper across the table and on to the floor as I discarded it, revealing one toy after another. Nearly every card I opened had a badge attached which I immediately pinned to myself until I clanked when I moved, and everyone kept calling me 'birthday boy'. I was delirious with joy. Uncle David told me I didn't have to go to school that day, that I could stay at home and play with my new toys all day long. From the moment the others left I just sat in the midst of my booty, staring at them, playing with them, pulling them apart and putting them back together.

One of them was a little brown bear, which sat beside me all day, sharing the excitement. The staff just left me alone to wallow in my happiness.

When the others came back from school in the afternoon everyone started to prepare for a birthday party, the first I'd ever been to. It felt so strange to be the centre of attention. We played pass-the-parcel and stick-the-tail-on-the-donkey, and everyone became overexcited and loud. This was a party like the ones I used to hear about in the school playground, the ones I never got to see for myself, and it was every bit as exciting as anything I'd ever imagined.

Suddenly all the lights went out and I felt a stab of fear in my stomach. All the bright colours of the decorations and the presents disappeared and everyone fell silent. A wave of panic threatened to overwhelm me. I couldn't work out what was going on. It was like being back in my bedroom with no light, and then I saw the glow coming in through the door. Uncle David was bringing in the cake from the kitchen. It was big enough for everyone in the house to have a piece. It had 'Happy Birthday, Kevin' written across it in icing, with eight candles. They all began to sing 'Happy Birthday' to me as I blew out the candles.

The lights came back on and I started to cry. Eight years of pent-up emotion and bottled unhappiness poured out uncontrollably and all I could think was that I missed the brothers and sisters I hadn't seen for a year. I felt so happy and imagined them still trapped at home with Gloria and Dennis, with all the shouting and hitting, the violence and the unhappiness, the darkness and the hunger, the dirt and the smells. It was all too much for me to cope with and the tears streamed out.

Uncle David scooped me up and carried me upstairs to

the bedroom. He gave me a cuddle and assured me everything was all right. When he told me that, I believed it was true.

Life at Yarborough gave me a great sense of freedom. Bit by bit I was becoming a normal, inquisitive child, a happy child, playful and looking for adventure. We often played football in the backyard. If a ball was kicked over the fence into the lane the person who kicked it had to get it. We were playing one day when I gave an almighty kick and the ball flew straight over. I clambered up the fence and when I got to the top I had a good look around. Slowly I stood straight up, suddenly filled with confidence and happiness. I spread my arms out like I was free and standing on top of a mountain. All around was the green of the trees and I felt a breeze on my face. This, I thought to myself, is what freedom feels like. I felt dizzy with excitement, lost my concentration and fell to the ground, breaking my arm. I had to be taken to the local hospital to be plastered up. I didn't care. A broken arm was a small price to pay for finally being free.

5

A Chance

With the move to a new home came an inevitable move to a new school. This one was not far from the home and was called Baldwin's Hill. To get there we just had to walk down the unmade lane beside Yarborough to the next road. It was a very different atmosphere to Wolsey Junior, more like an old-fashioned Victorian village school and I immediately felt safe and comfortable there. I was kitted out with a brand-new uniform and sat next to a boy called Guy Monson who showed me around and we became firm friends. I was so happy I thought I might burst. Here I had everything I'd been missing at home. At Yarborough I was secure and well cared for, never afraid I would be hit or humiliated in any way, and at school I was as clean and smart as every other boy, with a real best friend of my own. Just to have a regular supply of clean underpants was a luxury, let alone clean bedding. I no longer smelled different to everyone else, even though I still had problems with bed-wetting. No one would have dreamt of calling me 'tramp' at Baldwin's Hill. I'd become a part of normal life, no longer odd and different or an easy target for anyone who wanted to give someone a hard time.

My friendship with Guy grew and he started to invite me back to his home to play after school. His house was a cosy little bungalow down another bumpy lane, buried amongst high hedges and trees, a short walk from the school in another direction. It was difficult to imagine that we were still in the outskirts of a town when we had farmland just across the way and no signs of any traffic. I met his mum, Gini, who was everything a mum should be. She and her husband were divorced. She was bringing Guy up on her own, and she was doing it brilliantly. She couldn't have been more different to Gloria. She worked in the media in some way, I think it was public relations, and the house was full of books and stacks of magazines I'd never heard of before like *Punch*, *Private Eye* and *New Statesman*.

Our friendship grew and I started to go there for sleep-overs. Sometimes when I stayed there for the night Guy and I would creep outside after we were supposed to be in bed, slipping through his bedroom window and down the lane in the eerie darkness, being adventurous as all boys are, only sometimes we only succeeded in frightening ourselves so much we had to scuttle back to the bedroom and spend the rest of the night imagining green monsters knocking on the windows. The only thing that spoiled these nights for me was the fear that I might wet the bed and I would try to make myself sleep lightly in order to be aware of the danger signs like dreaming about a toilet.

The staff at Yarborough gave us a great deal of freedom and we were allowed to go out and about in the surrounding roads and woods as long as we were with older children. *Grease* was a popular film at the time and we all used to imitate their way of dressing, walking about with our collars up, feeling like real little dudes. There was a pond not too far from the house, surrounded by trees and some distance from the nearest houses. It was a cold winter and the pond had frozen over. A group of us, including some girls and my roommates, Chris and Mark, decided to go down there and slide on the ice, even though we'd been told it was out of bounds. I guess all children will be tempted by the forbidden occasionally and the lure of that smooth expanse of slippery ice was too much for us. We were tentative to start with, gingerly putting our feet on to the surface to test its strength. Once we knew it would take our weight our courage grew and we ventured further and further from the edge as we played our games, laughing and falling over, grabbing hold of one another and skating around as best we could in our boots and shoes.

Chris was being particularly daring. He'd spotted a barrel on the other side that must have been floating in the pond when the ice came and was now stuck fast. As he became braver he was sliding closer and closer to the barrel. As more of us poured on to the ice it held fast. The odd cracking noises around the edges didn't seem to develop into anything serious and so we became less and less cautious.

The presence of the barrel must have weakened the ice on that side of the pond. We heard a crack and splash at the same time as Chris's shout. We looked over and saw him disappear from sight. Before we could do anything he'd bobbed back to the surface. Other people were screaming and some had scrambled back to the bank, pursued by the sounds of cracking ice, and were already running back up the hill towards Yarborough to get help. Chris was flailing around, trying to find something to hold on to, but there was nothing, only ice that was too slippery to grip. The weight of the water in his clothes was pulling him down and I could see he wouldn't be able to stay up long enough for Uncle David to be found and to run down from the house. Even when he got there it would take a few minutes before he was able to work out a way to reach Chris. An adult as heavy as him would also be much more likely than one of us to go through the ice somewhere else. I didn't pause to weigh up the odds for long, I just knew we had to hold on to Chris to stop him going under, and then we could try to drag him out.

I walked gingerly towards him and felt the ice cracking beneath my feet. I realized I had to distribute my weight more widely. It was instinctive. I lay down as close as I could get to the hole he'd made, shouting at Mark to grab my legs. The freezing cold water from the surface immediately soaked through my clothes to my skin. I reached out my hands and yelled at Chris to catch hold of them. He lifted his hands from the ice and tried to stretch, but he just floundered more and slipped further away. His face was going under and then coming back. His teeth were chattering and I could feel the same piercing cold that must have been enveloping him.

I wriggled closer, the ice making ominous clicking sounds all around, and Mark edged forward behind me, his fingers digging desperately into my ankles. Everyone else was on the bank screaming advice or just panicking. Chris lunged at me again but missed and disappeared beneath the surface once more. This time I didn't think he would have the strength to come up again. I plunged my arm into the water and grabbed a handful of his clothes. It was hard to get a grip when my fingers were so cold they had gone numb.

'Pull me back!' I shouted at Mark who skidded and slipped as he put all his strength into hauling me away from the edge of the hole, while I clung on to his brother with frozen fingers. Mark somehow managed to get enough strength to pull me back a few feet and Chris began to come up out of the water. Every time he put his elbows on to the ice it would crack beneath the weight and plunge him down into the water again, but at least we were edging towards the shore. Gradually, as we moved away from the barrel the ice became stronger and I was able to haul his top half out, but from the waist down he was still below the surface. He seemed to be almost unconscious, his eyes dazed and every part of him shivering and shaking as he coughed up filthy pond water. He hardly seemed to have any strength at all. It was like trying to lift a dead weight. Mark kept pulling and now the screams of the others were turning to cheers of encouragement.

By the time we were dragging him on to firm ground several members of staff had come running down from the house with blankets and towels. I knew we were going to be in trouble for this, but I was so relieved just to be back on solid land and to have a dry towel wrapped round me that I didn't care about anything else.

When we got back to the house Chris was taken off for a hot bath and the rest of us had to explain what had happened. The others gave a vivid account of the rescue and that evening Mark and I were given extra helpings of pudding, as well as being told off for disobeying orders. Once the excitement was over and I had time to reflect over the adventure, I felt pleased to have accomplished something so good, even if it was in desperation. I felt proud of myself and it was a wonderful feeling. Perhaps I wasn't quite as useless as Gloria had been telling me.

6

A Lesson Learned

Although we were all very happy at Yarborough, we still used to talk about running away. It just seemed like the right thing to do, especially whenever *Huckleberry Finn* or *Stig of the Dump* had been on the television. It wasn't that we wanted to get away from the house; it was just that a life of freedom, sleeping under the stars at night and being free to wander wherever you wanted during the day, seemed so romantic. We wanted to be masters of our own destiny, or at least we thought we did. Whenever a programme like that was on the staff would be extra vigilant, knowing that at least a few of us would try to clamber out through the windows after dark. Once or twice I was one of the escape party and we were actually successful, but we were always back within a few hours, having realized that we weren't going to be finding a paddle ship like Huck's anywhere near East Grinstead, and that life was better when you had access to table tennis and billiard tables, not to mention a warm bed.

New children would come and go from time to time and one girl, Kimberley, who came for a few weeks to give her parents a rest, seemed to be slightly retarded. She couldn't talk very much but she made a big effort to communicate with me, mainly in 'umms' and 'ahhs', but always with a big smile. I rather liked her and we got on well. She was a big girl, probably fifteen or sixteen years old, and looked more like one of the staff than one of the children. For some reason Mark and Chris didn't like her at all. She was too different for them and they really didn't want anything to do with her. They seemed to find her irritating and I noticed they were picking on her sometimes, being spiteful, calling her names and egging her on.

Because she was a bit simple she made an easy target, and they gradually grew more vindictive, like children sometimes do when they find an easy victim. They got into trouble about it more than once but it didn't stop them. They just couldn't resist the temptation to tease her when they got her on her own.

One evening I was walking past the games room when I heard noises coming from inside. I looked in to see what was happening and saw Kimberley cowering in a corner of the room like a frightened animal, with Chris and Mark taunting her. The boys were gleefully sliding knives across the floor at her, making her wide-eyed with terror. I had visions of the knife that was thrown at my brother, but now I knew this shouldn't be part of normal life.

'Leave her alone,' I said.

'Go away,' Mark said. They were having too good a time to stop and they certainly didn't see why they should do what I told them.

'Leave her alone,' I repeated, certain that what they were doing was wrong and that Kimberley needed help.

I guess they didn't like having their authority challenged in front of their victim and they turned their attentions on to me. They both picked up billiard cues and moved towards me threateningly. 'Go away,' Mark said again.

I definitely wasn't going to go anywhere now or I would

have marked myself out as a coward for ever. In fact the thought of deserting Kimberley didn't enter my head. As they advanced on me I picked up a billiard ball and hurled it at Chris with all my strength. It was a brilliant shot, hitting him square in the middle of his forehead. There was a loud crack of ivory on bone and he crumpled to the ground. He lay still, with no sign of life. Mark glanced at his brother and then rushed at me, brandishing the cue furiously. I felt a surge of anger and, grabbing another ball, drew back my arm to throw again when I felt a pair of adult arms wrapping round me and I was lifted off the ground. The ball fell from my fingers.

'Calm down, Kevin,' Uncle David instructed me, as someone else ran over to tend to Chris on the floor where he was still out cold.

The room was suddenly full of staff, followed by the other children, all of them sensing some excitement and eager to see what was happening. Kimberley was still whimpering in the corner, frightened now by all the shouting and rushing around. I'd lost all control of my temper by then. I was kicking and screaming, shouting and swearing, memories of a hundred past confrontations with Gloria and Dennis going through my mind. Uncle David carried me to another room, still telling me to calm down and pinning me firmly in the crook of his arm so I couldn't escape.

Eventually I managed to get control of myself and sat, shaking, as Uncle David gave me a glass of milk and asked what had happened. I described the scene I'd witnessed.

'Why didn't you come and get me?' he asked.

I shrugged. It hadn't occurred to me. That would have been like snitching. It seemed like a situation I had to deal with myself.

'You mustn't take the law into your own hands,' he counselled.

I listened and nodded because I respected him, but it didn't sound right to me. I thought that if you wanted to get anything done in life, if you wanted to survive, you did have to take the law into your own hands. If you were hungry and no one would feed you, then you had to steal food from the fridge at night; that was how I believed life worked. If someone fell through the ice you did your best to get them out. If you wanted someone to stop doing something you had to make them. What he was saying didn't make sense to someone who had spent the early years of his life with no one he could turn to for help. I thought it was better that I followed my instincts and used my initiative in a difficult situation. But I didn't say anything.

My punishment for knocking Chris out was to be sent to my bedroom straight after getting back from school the next day. It wasn't too serious, compared to the sort of punishments I had been used to at home, and I suppose it was fair because I could have done Chris a serious injury. But it was also humiliating. My meal was brought up to me. It was a sunny evening and I stood at the window watching the others playing outside in the garden. I could see that Chris had a lump the size of a chicken's egg on his forehead, surrounded by a huge bruise.

Even though I'd been punished I didn't regret what I'd done. It still seemed like the right thing to do under the circumstances. A few days later I came back from school and found Kimberley had moved from the home. I was upset that I hadn't been given a chance to say goodbye.

7
Going Home

A few months after settling into Yarborough I was told that I could start making weekend visits home. I had mixed feelings about this. I still missed my brothers and sisters, but I had no wish to spend any time with Gloria and Dennis, sinking back into the noise, the dirt and the aggression that I was so relieved to have escaped from. Given a choice I would have preferred to stay with Guy or my friends at Yarborough. I wasn't, however, being offered an option and I didn't feel able to say that I didn't want to see my own family. The visits were to become a regular part of my routine every other weekend. Staff from Yarborough would drop me off on a Saturday or Sunday morning and then pick me up in the late afternoon. It was just a question of enduring the hours in between.

Now that I'd been away and experienced another life, I felt a real outsider at home. The house felt small and claustrophobic compared to Yarborough and there was nothing to do, no billiard or table-tennis tables, no toys or games. I had new clothes now and had grown used to living in nice, clean places. I had seen how the rest of the world lived, which made the sights and sounds of my own family all the more oppressive and depressing. Whereas I had once accepted life amongst them as natural, I could see that it was anything but. Now I was seeing them in almost the same light as other visitors to the house, like welfare workers and debt collectors, and the sight did not make me proud to be one of them.

I was doing well at my new school so I could read and write and I was used to being able to talk to people without being shouted at. I was used to groups of people interacting normally, not all yelling at once. It was a culture shock to have to go back to the old way of living, even for a day at a time.

When I arrived back at the tin house I felt completely different to the rest of them. Nothing in the way they behaved to one another had changed from the moment I'd been taken away, over a year before. Everything looked the same, sounded the same and smelt the same, only to me it seemed worse because I was no longer accustomed to it, and there was the same chaos everywhere. Everyone was still screaming and shouting at one another, with Gloria at the centre of the storm all the time. Whereas at Yarborough there were dozens of different things to do, at home there was only the television blaring away. I didn't know what to do with myself from the moment I arrived to the moment I left. It was just a question of waiting for the hours to pass.

Robert and Brenda, who had been little more than babies when I left, were both getting older and so there were two more mouths to feed and two more mouths to shout. The only difference now was that Gloria and Dennis couldn't hit me, because there was always someone coming to pick me up within a few hours. They knew that if they had bruised or cut me it would have been spotted and they would have been in trouble. I was protected from them, but that added to my separateness, as if an invisible glass shield was keeping me from them. I was grateful for that protection, but it made things more uncomfortable. I would play with my brothers and sisters all day, but be hugely relieved when it was time to go back to my friends at Yarborough.

To make matters worse, Dennis had had to give up work. It had been discovered that he was epileptic. He'd suffered a fit while working on the lines, so British Rail had laid him off with a bit of redundancy money, which he was using to buy more and more drink in his attempt to escape from the horrible reality of life at home. The more he drank the sadder he became.

When I was ten years old, two years after arriving at Yarborough, Uncle David gave me the worst piece of news possible. He told me I was going back home on a permanent basis. Gloria and Dennis must somehow have been able to convince the authorities they had mended their ways, that they were now fit parents for me, that they wouldn't be abusing me any more. How anyone looking at the state of the house and them could have believed that I will never know. Even then I didn't for one moment believe that anything would be different once I was back in their power. Although they were being nice to me when I visited, and I liked seeing my brothers and sisters, I didn't want to go back to living in dirt, with no decent regular meals or drinks, no lights in the bedrooms and all the other restrictions. I was sure that once they had me back in the house everything would return to how it had been when I was little and I would lose all the advantages that my stay at Yarborough had given me. I was so happy where I was I would have stayed there for ever if they'd allowed it. I'd grown used to mixing with other children and I wasn't sure that I would be able to cope with the constant screaming and shouting again, let alone the physical and mental torture.

It's hard to imagine how the authorities could have thought that things would be any better. There were now six active children to feed and virtually no income at all. We didn't have any breadwinner in the whole family and it was obvious, even to us children, that Dennis had a drink problem. The pressures were bound to be building up again, so why did they think it was the right place for me to be?

When the time came for me to leave Yarborough, Uncle David gave me a toy car to take with me. He hugged me tightly as we were saying goodbye.

'You're a very special boy, Kevin,' he said, 'with a kind heart. Nobody can take that away from you.'

I hugged him back, said goodbye to all the others, who had been my family for two years, and was taken out to the car by a social worker. I felt like I was being driven to my execution. I was scared, my stomach churning round and round, visions of my earlier life flashing into my mind and taunting me. The journey to New Addington seemed to take for ever. It was teatime when we arrived and as we walked up the path Gloria opened the door to greet us, the other children milling around her legs. She was being as loud and friendly as she knew how. The social worker only stayed a few minutes and I went through to see my father in the kitchen. A terrible air of sadness hung around him. It was as if life had finally defeated him, as if he'd tried everything he could think of to make a success of things and had realized that none of it was going to work, that there was now nothing that could save him from the reality of the life we were all living except the gin bottle.

To begin with things weren't as bad as I'd anticipated. I

went back to my old school, although I didn't remember any of the other children very clearly, and my experiences at Yarborough meant I was now able to mix more easily with both boys and girls. When I was tiny I'd looked on all women and girls with fear, now I realized I didn't have to do that, that they could be my friends too.

Within a couple of weeks, however, things had slipped badly downhill. Gloria gave my new clothes and toys away to Wayne. If I protested that anything was mine she'd go mad at me, so I learned to keep quiet and never complain. My father's drinking was a constant strain on everyone. Although he no longer had a job, he couldn't stand to be in the house all day so he used to go up to Battersea in London and just sit in the Mason's Arms, a pub by the bridge over the Thames, where all his old workmates used to meet. He was too shy to make new friends, but he had to escape from Gloria's ranting and raving for at least part of the day. He would always dress up in his suit to go out and at weekends or in school holidays we'd all start screaming and shouting at him as he left the house, begging him to take us with him. If I didn't get picked, after making so much fuss, I'd have to scarper out of the house the moment he did, or Gloria'd beat me half to death for trying to get away from her.

Sometimes I would be picked to go with him, and I loved those days. There would always be an argument before he left, but once we were out of the house a sort of peace settled on us both. The Mason's Arms was a dark, smoky pub and I'd sit in a corner seat with an orange squash, while he sat at the bar with a pint. Occasionally, he'd glance over to check I was all right, or one of his mates would send me on an errand, like buying a newspaper. I knew that on those days I was safe because I was away from Gloria. Dennis and

I would go up together on the train, because he still had a concessionary ticket which allowed him to travel for free. We could even sit in the first-class carriages if it was outside rush hour, but I always had to be quiet and on my best behaviour. I had to sit straight and look respectable and he would hiss instructions at me from between gritted teeth. But I didn't mind that, as long as I was out of the house and safe.

On one of the return trips home, after Dennis had been in the pub, drinking from before midday until after six in the evening, we headed for the train to Victoria station as usual. From there we could get a fast train to East Croydon, then a bus on to New Addington. It was the rush hour still and as we made our way across Victoria there were people rushing everywhere. They reminded me of ants hurrying away when water is poured on them. We managed to get two seats in first class, but we weren't supposed to be there at that time of day so Dennis told me to sit up straight and keep quiet. The corridor outside our compartment was packed with people anxious to get home. I felt uncomfortable, sure that they were wondering what we were doing there. I looked over at Dennis and saw he was starting to shake uncontrollably. The other people in the compartment became aware of it too. Soon it was too serious for them to politely ignore and they got up, confused and embarrassed, not knowing what to do. I'd seen it many times before and asked them to give him space. He was throwing his arms about, bumping into the people in the other seats. I tried to loosen his tie for him, but my fingers weren't strong enough to undo the knot. A man offered to help and I told him what needed to be done.

'You need to undo his tie and his top shirt buttons,' I said.

'He needs to lie on the floor, on his side so he doesn't choke.'

The man asked another passenger to help and together they laid my father out on the floor of the compartment as he jerked and frothed. Outside I could hear a voice coming over the loudspeakers: 'If there's a doctor on the station, would you please make yourself known to a member of British Rail staff.'

The train remained stationary and the crowd around us waited with barely concealed annoyance for something to be done so they could get back to their homes. A few minutes later a doctor came into the compartment and checked Dennis over.

'He suffers from epilepsy,' I explained, trying to be helpful.

The doctor nodded his understanding and did his best to make my father comfortable as we waited for the fit to pass. There was nothing else we could do as the minutes ticked past agonizingly slowly. As Dennis came round things started to get back to normal. The doctor helped him back up into his seat and other people sat down cautiously around him, trying not to look nervous. For a man as shy as Dennis it must have been a horrible experience to become such a public spectacle. I sat back on my seat and noticed everyone staring down at me, the same way the children and teachers had done so often at school. I guess they were now wondering what we were doing in a first-class compartment. I felt uneasy and averted my eyes outside the windows to escape their stares, but there were even more people peering up at me from the platform. This time it seemed as though I was looking down at them, but it didn't make me feel any better about it. I glanced at my father, who was still getting his composure back and avoiding my eyes. I turned back to the window and poked my tongue out as far as I could make it go. The faces on the other side of the glass didn't look too pleased, but then the crowd began to break up and the train prepared to start its journey.

I was used to Dennis having fits, but not in public places. Sometimes they gave me a chance to exact a modest revenge on him for all the times he had hurt me or turned a blind eye when Gloria did. I'd learned that if he was having one and I put my hand up to his face, it would completely freak him out. Sometimes, if he'd been giving me a beating and I was feeling spiteful towards him, I used to do that on purpose, just to punish him for what he did to me. Sometimes I suspected he was putting the fits on just to get out of an argument with Gloria – even she found it difficult to continue shouting abuse at a man when he was lying on the floor frothing at the mouth.

On the walk home from the bus stop each day he'd always pick up a half bottle of gin in the off-licence, and spend the evening standing in the kitchen with it, listening to the same Elvis tracks I'd been hearing all my life. As the evenings wore on he would turn up the volume to drown out every other noise in the house. To buy those bottles each day must have cost more than the rest of our household expenses added together; and he was smoking as well. Even at my young age I could see that it would be impossible for us to ever climb out of the pit we'd fallen into as long as Dennis had such a bad habit. The only hope was going to be for me to find ways to earn money myself which I could keep away from him and Gloria and use to buy food for the rest of us. But I couldn't see any way that I could do that with any regularity for at least another couple of years. I was completely trapped and pined terribly for Uncle David, Yarborough and all my friends in East Grinstead. When I had been there I had been able to be a child, if only for two years.

8

Sliding Downhill

When I first arrived back at my old school I must have seemed to the other children more like one of them, but they could soon see that I wasn't, that I was still one of the tramps.

My new teacher, Mrs Larkin, was very kind to me. She was slim and softly spoken. She seemed to me to be everything that a mother should be and I was always desperate to please her and win her approval. I could tell that she liked me; that she could see through the façade I put up to the person underneath. As I started to look and smell like a tramp once more, my clothes obviously out of fashion and down at heel, the other children began to distance themselves and the taunting began again. They would cuss at me whenever I passed, in the playgrounds or the corridors, the classrooms and the changing rooms; there was no escaping their taunts. They would shout insults about my mother; insults that I knew were based in truth. Whatever I might have felt about Gloria in private, however, I still believed I had to defend my family against the outside world and I would attack anyone who bad-mouthed her. I'd inherited a bad temper from her, which often got me in trouble with the teachers, who always felt I was an unruly child. There just didn't seem to be any break from the stresses and strains, from the moment I woke in the morning to the moment I fell back into unconsciousness at night I was fighting or being attacked by someone. Even when I was asleep I wasn't safe because of the nightmares. The stress built up inside me like a tight spring and every so often I would lose control.

As my social acceptability went downhill, so did my schoolwork. I found it impossible to concentrate in class, which also got me into more trouble with the teachers, and it was impossible to do homework at the house in the evenings since there wasn't a single quiet room and no clear surfaces to work on. With no light in the bedrooms I couldn't even go there. I've heard of children from poor families in the Third World having to sit underneath street lamps in order to work after dark because there is no light strong enough in their homes. I can understand exactly what drives them, but in the suburbs of South London there is no such option. My time was taken up with dealing with my hunger, hiding from Gloria and Dennis, not making a noise so as to avoid a beating. The work just didn't get done and my results slid back down to the bottom of the class.

I was hungry all the time because we always left the house in the morning without breakfast and then had to wait for lunchtime in order to use the council tokens we'd been given. I found it impossible to resist the temptation to steal bits of food from other children's lunch boxes during the morning to try to stave off the pains in my stomach.

Everyone knew it was me who was stealing and so I became branded as a thief as well as a tramp. I regretted having to do it, but I was just so hungry and the boxes of food looked so tempting. I would try to remember Uncle David's words about not taking the law into my own hands, but then the hunger would take over again. I don't think it is possible for a small child to resist taking food if they're that hungry. I don't believe it is a test that they should ever be put to or judged for.

At home the television was always on, competing with the shouting and banging, and the images I saw on the screen provided a desperately needed escape route from reality for me. I'd sit for hours on the grimy floor, amongst the piles of dirty washing and litter, attempting to be as small and quiet as possible in order not to attract Gloria's attention, trying to lose myself in the programmes that showed me a better life. Even basic kids' stuff like *Playaway* on Sunday afternoons provided a simple escape before bath time.

But the best programmes all came from America. They had a sense of fun and drama and simple storylines of good versus evil. My favourites were *Mork and Mindy*, *Starsky and Hutch*, *Kojak*, *Dukes of Hazard*, *Chips* and of course *Huckleberry Finn*, where everyone was always happy, doing whatever they wanted to do. Good always triumphed over adversity and everyone had something witty to say in every situation. Everything seemed so much better in America, bigger, freer, more relaxed and more open. But it was always hard to lose yourself in the programmes when there were so many people around making so much noise and trying to pick fights.

Often, when I was down, I'd imagine myself going to America, the land of Huckleberry Finn. I had a fantasy that one day my real parents would turn up at the house, explain there'd been a terrible mix-up at the hospital and take me away. I imagined they came from America and were planning to take me back there for a life like the ones I'd seen on television. One day I knew I would go there and it was that thought that kept me going. When everything around you is against you, you have to have a dream and mine was America. As soon as the credits rolled on one programme I couldn't wait for the next one to start. Well-meaning people sometimes criticize children for watching too much television, accusing them of being 'couch potatoes', but in families like mine the small screen was the only place where I would find any intellectual stimulation at all. The idea of reading a book was laughable and there was nothing else, just the endless repetition of Elvis songs in the kitchen, cigarettes and gin. At least television gave me a glimpse of what was possible in life, gave me some hope that there might, one day, be a light at the end of the tunnel.

What little money we had coming in from the state was getting used up earlier and earlier every week, leaving us having to scrounge whatever we could get from other people. Sometimes there wasn't even enough money in the house to buy Gloria and Dennis their cigarettes and we would be sent out to search for butt ends in the gutters or on the floors of shops. We would bring our booty home to them, like the kids in *Oliver Twist* returning to Fagin's lair, and they would then extract the tiny amounts of unburned tobacco and roll it in Rizla cigarette papers just to feed their habits for another day, until they could afford another packet.

Life at Yarborough soon began to seem like a distant dream; something that had happened to someone else and not to me. With six hungry, unruly children and two unbalanced adults all in one small pre-fabricated house there could never ever be any space or peace for any of us, no time to recover ourselves from the constant fights and arguments. We hardly ever went out, since there was nowhere to go, so we were rubbing up against one another all the time. Weekends, especially Sunday afternoons, were the worst and the school holidays at Christmas, Easter and during the summer, seemed to stretch on for ever. There was no escape for any of us. At least on normal school days we could get out of the house and away from one another for a few hours. However bad things were at school, it was always better than being at home. Wayne and I just tried to stay out of the house for as long as possible each day, desperately trying to think of ways to earn money for food to fill our permanently empty stomachs.

9

Fighting to Survive

Wayne, Sharon and Julie now tended to side with Gloria and Dennis against me if there was a fight. I could understand why they did that; I was bigger now and more able to take care of myself, and if they sided with me they were likely to be beaten for their trouble. But their defection made things harder for me and sometimes I hated them for the small amounts of attention they would get that I was denied, particularly Wayne and Brenda. Sometimes Gloria would let the others go outside to play, but tell me I had to stay in. So I'd have to sit by the window, watching them playing, just like the time at Yarborough, but when Gloria did this there was no justice or reason to it, just spite.

I must have got on Gloria's nerves almost from the moment I walked back through the door from East Grinstead, and she was soon unable to resist beating me whenever I came near her. I was simply too annoying for her to be able to bear. Because I was bigger now I was even more determined not to cry, and that seemed to infuriate her further; she must have seen it as some new kind of defiance of her power over me, because she would keep going, hitting and punching and shouting until eventually I was unable to hold the tears back any longer. My father would also join in the beatings, driven to distraction by her goading over his 'fucking son' and her accusations that he wasn't doing anything about disciplining me. To avoid arguing with her he would just lay into me for whatever imagined crime I'd committed. What I couldn't understand was that the majority of the time I didn't do anything wrong. Why would I, knowing what terrible punishments I would receive if I did?

The bruises rose all over my body, but she wasn't happy just to abuse me physically. As she did it she would constantly be shouting into my ear, her face an inch away from mine, 'Kevin's gay! Kevin's gay! He's gay, he's gay, he's gay!' All the time biting, pinching, kicking and punching me to give force to her words. 'You fucking queer!' Just as she had done a few years earlier.

I had no idea why she thought that. I don't know if I looked a bit feminine or whether she just picked it as a random insult. I had a rough idea what it meant, but I couldn't see why it applied to me. I wondered if there was something wrong with me that she knew about and I didn't. Was I gay? I would ask myself.

Now Dennis was at home all the time, if he wasn't in the pub, the friction between them increased to a permanent boiling point. When we were at school and there was no one else to attack, they would go for each other. One day, when I came home from school I found them fighting each other in the front room. She didn't fight like a woman. It was like watching two men in a pub brawl. They were grabbing hold of one another and punching as hard as they could, just like the staged fighting I saw in the American cop series, except that with Dennis and Gloria I could see the damage that was being done. They were pulling each other's hair, sending chairs and clothes flying as they ricocheted around the room. The other children were all screaming at them to stop, panic-stricken at the sight of their parents ripping each other to pieces.

I joined in the shouting, trying to make them listen to reason and back off one another; sure they were going to keep going until one of them was killed. My voice must have got through to them because they paused for a moment, his eyes dazed with drink and from the blows she'd landed on him, her spitting with anger, and they turned on me. Suddenly united in their anger they grabbed me and pinned me down, punching, kicking and biting me as the others screamed at them to stop. It was as if their hatred of me united and overcame their anger with each other. The screams of the other children grew louder. They must have thought I was now going to be killed, but eventually the pair of them exhausted themselves and I was able to crawl out of the room and up to my bedroom.

Such incidents were becoming more and more frequent and more and more violent with every passing day. Sometimes Gloria would come up with new ways to inflict pain on me. She had an old-fashioned, top-loading washing machine, which had an automated mangle on top. It consisted of two rollers that would squeeze the excess water out of the clothes to make them dry quicker. Wayne and I used to play a game of daring one another to touch the rollers when they were turning. Catching us doing it one day she became so incensed she pushed my fingers into the mangle. The pain was instant as the rollers pulled my fingers relentlessly through, crushing them.

'Mummy, no!' I screamed, over and over, hysterical with fear, believing I was going to lose my fingers. The more I screamed the harder she pushed. My yells must have been louder and more urgent than usual because Dennis appeared beside us, barging her aside and pulling my fingers free before the joints were crushed beyond mending. I learnt not to call her Mummy any more.

As everything in my day-to-day life grew grimmer, I kept one lifeline to the outside world open. I was still in touch with Guy and Gini Monson, the friends I'd made in East Grinstead. We'd exchange letters and every so often Gini would come and fetch me for a day out with them. Gloria would open Gini's letters before she gave them to me and tease me with them; no one else in our family ever received handwritten letters, but she could do nothing to stop these treats without giving away to outsiders how spiteful she was being to me in the privacy of the family. When I was with Gini and Guy I would go along with the pretence that everything was all right at home because I didn't want anyone feeling sorry for me, and because if Gloria knew I'd been saying things about her that would be another excuse to beat me. I suspect Gini guessed from the bruises I often carried, but if she asked about them I'd just say I fell. I'm sure she must have known something terrible was happening to me at home, but she respected my privacy and didn't ask any questions I wouldn't have wanted to answer. She just let me know that she would always be there for me if I needed a friend. That meant an awful lot to me.

I loved my stays with them. The only things that spoiled them for me was that I was still wetting the bed. Although Gini would never be angry with me for something like that and would help me clear it up as discreetly as possible, it was still mortifying. My relationship with Guy was not as strong as it had been when I was at Yarborough and Baldwin's Hill. He was moving ahead at school, like most children of our age, whereas I was now slipping backwards. Each visit showed that we had less and less in common. I was becoming different again and there was no hiding that fact. As the gap widened between us I realized I was actually going to their house more because of my friendship with Gini than my friendship with her son. She was almost like a guardian to me, letting me talk and showing me that there was a world out there in which parents were kind to their children, supported them and did all the right things for them. But even when we were talking I still didn't tell her how badly things were going at home; I wouldn't have dared, in case she said something to Gloria when she dropped me back. But I guess, deep down, she knew.

As well as wetting the bed, I was having nightmares again, just as I had when I was small, waking up in the night sweating and crying, the same images vivid in my mind. There were two in particular. One of them featured hordes of ants. It was like watching a film, but the picture kept changing with a jolt, focusing in closer and closer until it was a tight shot of one horrible ant and I would be jerked awake in a panic. In another there were a king and queen, sitting on tall chairs, having their heads chopped off. The same scenes came to me, over and over again. I could never get used to them. I could never escape.

10

Losing Control

The pressure kept building inside my head. At home there were the constant beatings and the taunting: 'Kevin's gay! Kevin's gay!' And at school more taunting: 'Lewis is a tramp! Tramp! Tramp!' Even when I was asleep I couldn't get away from the nightmares.

It was relentless, hammering away at my brain with no break or respite for weeks on end. Gloria must have been able to exercise some self-control because she hardly ever hit me anywhere where it would show. Although my body was covered in bruises, none of them were visible when I was dressed, so no one at school spotted them except at P.E., when they would be explained away. Most of the time no one took any notice and there was nobody I could turn to for help because I didn't dare to betray Gloria for fear of the repercussions.

Eventually I couldn't take any more and the volcano erupted. We were on our way to assembly and a boy who seemed to me to have everything in the world just wouldn't let up on me. He kept on chanting, 'Tramp, tramp, Lewis is a tramp!'

He pushed it and pushed it until my temper exploded in a vast, boiling eruption and all hope of self-control was gone. I flew at him, just as my mother would fly at me, not holding back any of my strength or anger, blind and deaf to everything except my desire to silence him. Every ounce of the frustration that had been building inside me went into the punches I landed on him. My anger gave me a strength way beyond my puny, malnourished frame's normal abilities. My opponent had not been expecting any sort of response and collapsed to the floor immediately, but I couldn't stop hitting him even though I already had him beaten. That must have been how Gloria felt whenever she started hitting me, just not able to stop, wanting to pour every tiny bit of anger and frustration and unhappiness out. There was screaming and crying all round and a teacher called Mr Robinson appeared behind me. He probably ordered me to stop but I was past responding to orders, just a ball of anger in action. He grabbed me, holding me tightly, like Uncle David had at Yarborough when I was going for Chris and Mark with the billiard balls. He propelled me along to the main hall where people were coming into assembly. Everyone was using the other door to avoid the mayhem I was causing as I fought and kicked all the way. He threw open the doors and we stumbled in, me still struggling with all my strength, him trying to calm me. I kept fighting and he forced me down on the ground to get more control, whispering in my ear for me to calm down. Eventually I realized I was overpowered and I stopped struggling. I lay on the floor suddenly exhausted and burst into tears. Looking up I could see that the assembly room was now full of children and teachers.

Every pair of eyes in the room turned to look down at me. By the time I'd managed to get control of my sobbing the whole room was silent, everyone's attention fixed on the problem child on the floor, everyone excited by the drama of the situation, grateful for the distraction from the tedium of the normal routine. Yet again I'd been singled out from the crowd and shown up to be something different, something bad and wild and uncontrollable. I just wanted to shrink away to nothing. I wanted to change places with anyone else in the room. I didn't want to be Kevin Lewis for a moment longer. I never wanted to be Kevin Lewis, I always wanted to be someone else, someone with hope and a future, not someone for whom there was no escape.

Even after such a dramatic scene and such a public humiliation, I had no choice but to pick myself up and keep going with my life, knowing now it was only a matter of time before the same thing happened again. My teacher, Mrs Larkin, seemed to understand a bit of what I was going through. She always spoke to me in such a kind voice and I used to fantasize that she was my mother, instead of Gloria. One day, after swimming, when we got back to the class, I was so hungry I stole some pieces of food from a lunch box. A little girl saw me and started to call me 'tramp'. She was a red-haired girl who suffered from asthma and I should have been able to control myself, but I panicked. I'd had a bad time with Gloria the night before and so I punched her. I panicked more and was shaking nervously, not knowing what was going to happen next. She started crying and Mrs Larkin came through to see what was happening. She asked me for an explanation and I had none. She got hold of me and I became scared and kneed her in the groin, the one person who'd shown me any kindness and affection. I immediately knew I'd done something terribly wrong.

Mrs Larkin looked at me with sad eyes. 'Is that it, Kevin?' she asked and I burst into tears. 'Come on,' she said. 'Head-master's office.'

I'd hit a teacher, and a woman as well, and I'd hit a little girl. I knew now I'd gone way beyond the line of acceptable behaviour. They couldn't possibly avoid punishing me for this, and in a way I wanted to be punished, because I'd hurt Mrs Larkin, who'd always been on my side. Maybe I was as bad a person as Gloria said I was.

In the headmaster's office I just kept saying 'sorry' but it was far too late for that. Someone was sent to fetch Gloria and I knew what I would be in for. I begged them not to, but I guess they had no choice.

When Gloria arrived in the headmaster's office she was acting the concerned parent. Even though I'd kicked her, Mrs Larkin gave me such a look of warmth as they all explained to Gloria what had happened and I just wished I could turn the clock back an hour, so I could put everything right. The headmaster said I was suspended. It was the worst possible verdict because it meant I'd be trapped at home with Gloria for days on end. I felt sick with fear. She continued to act like a model parent as we left the headmaster's office.

As we walked across the school playground behind our house Gloria took my hand. To anyone watching it could have looked like a firm maternal gesture, but her fingers just kept squeezing harder and harder and my arm was nearly pulled out of its socket as she dragged me towards home. By the time we were into the alley between the houses, and out of sight of both the road and the school, I was begging her to stop crushing my fingers, but she took no notice. She couldn't hold back her fury a moment longer and my head exploded as her fist crashed into it. The pain was blinding and I would have fallen to the ground if she hadn't been holding me up by the arm. She kept dragging me towards the house, smacking my legs and pinching my arms as I stumbled along, trying to clear my head and keep up. She seemed unable to summon enough violence to make herself feel any better, to relieve whatever pressure was building in her own head. A continuous stream of swear words poured from her mouth and I felt that I was in serious danger. I knew that as soon as I was behind the closed front door she'd lose all self-control, just as I had done with the boy at school and she might just kill me.

As we came out of the alley I managed to break free and ran as fast as I could in the opposite direction along King Henry's Road. I could hear her voice echoing down the road after me in a screech of frustrated fury, unconcerned who else might be able to hear in the surrounding houses.

'You'll be sleeping in the fucking bath tonight, you fucking little cunt, if you don't come back here, now!'

Sleeping in the bath was the least of my fears. I was sure I'd be dead long before it was time to go to sleep. I was filled with fear, from the roots of my hair to the soles of my fleeing feet. The traffic roared past as I ran on, past the anonymous rows of houses and the ugly tower blocks of flats. I glanced over my shoulder. She was still shouting at me to come back, but her voice was growing fainter and she wasn't following me. I got to the end of the road and looked around frantically for somewhere to hide, not just from her, but from anyone else who might feel it their duty to take me back to her. I headed off towards the woods around the golf course that Wayne and I sometimes played in, the ones I'd planned to hide in many years before. Crossing the busy road at the top of the hill I came out on to the open grass that played host to local football matches. There was a sweeping view across the green valley with tiny figures of golfers in the distance. I just wanted to get as far from the streets full of houses and cars as possible. I ran on until I came to the first line of trees and threw myself down beneath the bushes, panting, my chest aching with the effort of running so far and so fast, my heart thumping. My fingers still hurt from where she'd crushed them and my head was spinning from the first punch. I needed to rest for a while. Once I'd recovered I spent the rest of the afternoon mooching about under the cover of the trees. It was pleasant to be alone and not to have to deal with anyone else. I liked the tranquillity of the woods. I imagined I was Huckleberry Finn and that I had no home to go back to, that I could wander in any direction I chose, enjoying whatever adventures turned up. It felt good to rest for a while and just be free, even though I knew it couldn't last.

When the sun went in it started to feel colder and the valley, which had looked so green and inviting a few hours before, was now full of shadows. I wondered if I could make myself a shelter somewhere, like they did in television programmes. I was beginning to feel desperately hungry and tried to think where I might be able to find something to eat. Even the idea of Gloria's fat-soaked chips was starting to seem attractive.

The shapes of the trees began to merge into one another and, as the rest of the world outside the wood grew quieter, I could hear the rustling of leaves and branches all around me. I began to imagine what might be hiding in them, watching me, waiting to pounce. Something screeched in the trees above my head and something else rustled past my feet unseen. My heart pounded in my chest. I knew that if I went home I'd be beaten, but at least I'd be in the safety of my own home and I'd be able to crawl into my bed once she'd finished with me. There might be something to eat, even if it was only leftovers. God alone knew what would happen to me in the wood if I stayed out all night. Reluctantly, I made my way home, the headlights steadily passing as I dragged my feet back along the pavements I had been running on just a few hours before.

Gloria must have been watching for me from the window because she opened the front door as I came into view. She stood still and threatening in the doorway, leaving just enough room for me to squeeze silently past.

'Your fucking son is here!' she shouted through to Dennis in the kitchen, and shut the front door behind me.

He came out to look at me and I saw his face was covered in scratches. I guessed they'd been fighting again and the thought made me even more frightened. Everyone else had eaten their chips and mine were standing on the table, waiting for me. They were cold, the fat going solid on the edges, but I was so hungry I would have eaten anything. When I'd swallowed the last mouthful Dennis told me to go to bed so I wouldn't irritate Gloria any more. As I went past him on the way to the door he put his hand on my shoulder, as he sometimes did. It was as if he was trying to communicate with me but couldn't find the words. I tried to stop myself crying, but I couldn't. Even a gesture as small as that was more than I could bear. He lifted me up and put his arms around me, holding me tightly. For a few seconds I felt safe, even though I knew she was waiting in the background and that she'd still be there the next day, once he'd gone out to the pub to see his friends.

She left me alone that night and I slept soundly. Maybe she was tired out from fighting with everyone else. The next day I wasn't able to go to school because of the suspension and I knew she wouldn't be able to stand having me around the house all day. I was right. Every day of the suspension she laid into me with whatever she could find; her hand, her belt or a broken broomstick. Eventually she hurt me so badly that I couldn't crawl out of bed the following morning. I stayed in bed all day and that evening, when Dennis came home from the pub, I heard them talking downstairs. He came up to my room and lifted me gently out of the bed without saying a word, carrying me through into their bedroom where there was a light. He examined the marks on my body while she stood watching in the background with her arms folded. I could see they were both nervous about something.

It was a bad day for her to choose to damage me so noticeably because a social worker was due to call the following day. They only came by every two or three weeks, so usually she left me alone for the few days before a call was due in order to allow the bruises to fade. This time she'd left it too late, although my face was still unmarked. They were obviously worried that this time she'd gone too far. Dennis carried me back to my bed.

The next day she left me in bed, tucking the covers up under my chin, and told me not to pull the covers down, whatever happened.

'If you say anything to the lady you'll get the fucking stick once she's gone,' she warned, and I had no reason to doubt her word.

I heard the social worker arriving downstairs. Apart from Brenda and Robert, who were still too young for school, the other children were out, leaving the house reasonably quiet with just the noise of the television playing in the background. I could hear Gloria's loud voice downstairs pouring out all her complaints and moans. All visitors to the house got out as quickly as they possibly could. I just hoped that this time the woman would pull down my bedcovers before she went. If she did that then it wouldn't be my fault if she saw the marks, and then perhaps they'd send me back to Yarborough. I waited, my heart pounding, as the voices came closer up the stairs. Gloria had left the curtains drawn so it would be difficult for the woman to see anything without a light. She was telling the woman about how I was feeling poorly and the woman was making sympathetic noises.

They arrived in the bedroom and the social worker asked how I was. I said I was fine, far too scared to say anything else for fear of the reprisals that would come after she'd left. She obviously wanted to believe me, because if I was all right then she could get out of the house as fast as possible. I concentrated with all my strength, trying to will her to lift the sheets that hid my broken body, but I could see she was already backing out of the door, probably trying to escape the smell as much as anything else.

'I hope you get better soon, Kevin,' she said, and was gone, taking all my hopes of escape with her.

The following week I was back at school and Mrs Larkin was behaving as if the whole incident had never happened. She was in the middle of organizing a talent contest.

'What would you like to be in the contest, Kevin?' she asked.

'Worzel Gummidge,' I replied, knowing that Gloria would never let me do something like that. Worzel was a scarecrow character who had his own popular television series at the time. All day I felt really sad that I wouldn't be able to join in the fun with everyone else.

When the bell went at the end of school Mrs Larkin asked me to wait behind.

'Would you like me to help you with your costume, Kevin?' she asked.

She must have known that all the other children would be getting help from their parents, and guessed that Gloria and Dennis would not be up to that sort of challenge.

'It's all right, Miss,' I said, my eyes on the floor. 'I'm not allowed to enter the contest.'

'Okay,' she said, putting her hand on my head. 'Would you like me to have a word with your parents for you?'

'No!' I said, more sharply than I wanted to. I could just imagine how Gloria would turn on me if a teacher came to the house, and I didn't want Mrs Larkin to see the way we lived either. I thought that if she saw our house she'd see me as the other children in the school did; she would see that I was just a tramp, and not someone who was worth bothering with.

All the other children kept talking about what they were going to do and be in the contest, but no one asked me, so I didn't have to confess that I wasn't going to enter. It was coming to the end of my time at Wolsey Junior and I comforted myself with the thought that maybe things would be better at the next school.

A few days before the contest there was a knock at the door after school and Mrs Larkin was standing there when Gloria opened it. My heart sank and I slunk out of sight. The two of them stood talking on the doorstep and I stayed right out of the way, straining to hear what was going on. Mrs Larkin's voice was so quiet I couldn't hear what she was saying and Gloria didn't say anything to me after she'd gone. I knew better than to ask any questions. I was just relieved that the visit hadn't resulted in me getting a beating.

The next morning, during our break, Mrs Larkin asked me to stay behind.

'I've got something to show you,' she said, pulling a plastic carrier bag out from under her desk. Inside was a complete scarecrow outfit, with straw up the sleeves and patches all over. 'This is your costume for the contest tomorrow.'

'But –' I protested.

'It's all right.' She cut me short. 'Everything's been sorted out with your mother. But you'd better think up some lines to say if you want to win.'

That afternoon I wrote myself some lines. I spent ages over them, feeling like a real child, just like all the others instead of an outsider.

The next day the assembly hall was packed with parents, staff and visitors. I peeked through the side of the curtains, searching the sea of faces for Gloria and Dennis, but couldn't see either of them. I don't suppose I really expected them to be there and in a way I was relieved that they weren't, but it would have been nice to think they would see me doing something. Perhaps then they would have realized that I wasn't as completely useless as they were always saying I was. There was a real buzz in the air as we waited backstage to perform. I was in costume like everyone else. I was part of the action and everyone seemed to have forgotten that they despised me while I was hiding behind the Worzel Gummidge character. It felt almost unbearably good, like being back at Yarborough and part of a community. The straw itched horribly, but I didn't care.

When it came to my turn to perform I strode out on to the stage and there was a ripple of laughter at my costume before everyone fell silent, waiting to hear what I would say. I froze. I couldn't think of a thing to say, my head was empty, all my carefully prepared lines gone. I looked down at the front row and saw Mrs Larkin and Mr Robinson both looking up at me with encouraging smiles. After what seemed like an age words started to come out of my mouth, and then there was the most wonderful sound I'd ever heard. It was laughter, and it was for me. But it wasn't the cruel laughter I was used to. They weren't mocking me, they were enjoying my act. They were pleased with me. I tried a few more words and added an expression or two and movements I'd seen Worzel do on television and the laughter swelled up, lifting my confidence still further. There were people shouting out. It was uproar, such a happy noise. I was so thrilled they had trouble getting me off the stage. I could have stayed there all night. Eventually I took my bow and left, walking on air.

As soon as the show was over I ran home, so proud of myself and so excited by the experience.

I shouted to Gloria as I barged in through the front door, 'I had such a great time at the contest. You should have come!'

'Should?' she sneered, and I immediately knew I'd said the wrong thing. 'Should?'

I wiped the smile off my face and averted my eyes quickly. I ran straight upstairs to my bedroom to keep out of the way. Sitting on the edge of the bed, replaying everything that had happened in my head, I was unable to keep the smile from creeping back.

My time at Wolsey Junior was due to finish a few weeks later. Before I left Mrs Larkin gave us all a card with a twenty pence piece inside. My card simply said, 'Don't forget to count to ten before you react. Love, Mrs Larkin.'

11

Out to Work

School holidays were always difficult because it meant we were all imprisoned together in the house twenty-four hours a day. At least school gave us a breathing space of a few hours, even if it brought its own form of hell with it. When the holidays did come round I was always looking for excuses to go out and I was always hungry; so from the age of ten or eleven I started searching for ways to make some money to buy food for myself and for my brothers and sisters. This was around 1980.

It's hard to make money when you're that young, not only because there aren't that many jobs you are allowed to do, but because there are always people looking for ways to cheat children, trying to get something for nothing. I used to go to the local golf courses and offer my services as a caddy. Although golf courses are very pleasant places to be, particularly on fine days, caddying is hard work, particularly when you're still small and not as strong as you should be because of your appalling diet. I would spend all day lugging bags of clubs around for players and quite often they would realize they were out of cash at the end of the game. They would always have some excuse and would tell me where to find them later to collect my money. On several occasions I went searching for the addresses these men had given me, spending hours walking around the streets trying to remember exactly what the name was that they'd given me. Sometimes I'd have to take a guess and ring a doorbell, only to find it was the wrong place. It would have been so easy for these people just to give me the few pounds they owed me. It would have meant nothing to them; no more than the price of a small round of drinks, but it would have meant I could have bought some food. Every time someone pulled a stunt like that we just had to go another day without.

Even when I did manage to get my hands on some cash, there was never any point bringing it back into the house because Gloria or Dennis would take it off me to buy drink or cigarettes. They would always promise breezily to pay it back, but it never happened. So the moment any of us earned anything we'd buy sweets, or fish and chips, or whatever we could afford to stave off the pangs for a few hours. The people at the chippie up in the shopping precinct used to store their spare chippings of batter and sell it to us by the bag, which was cheap and filling.

If I did manage to get some money and didn't want to take it into the house, I would go home and wait outside in the phone booth opposite the house, trying to attract Wayne's or Sharon's attention, so we could all go down to the chippie together. It involved a lot of walking for a small boy; all the way back from the town or the golf courses with the money, and then all the way back up again with my brother and sisters. But the thought of food can drive a hungry child a long way.

Our diet was always terrible. Gloria didn't have any idea how to feed children. We lived pretty much totally on chips; we certainly didn't have any fresh fruit or vegetables. The chip pan was never washed; it just sat on the side in the kitchen, waiting for the next batch to be thrown in. The stale smell of frying clung to everything in the house and everyone who came there.

In the first summer holidays after I went back home from East Grinstead I also wanted to make enough money to buy myself a birthday present. Being at Yarborough had taught me how good it felt to be given something and I knew my parents wouldn't do it. So I decided to buy myself something, wrap it up in its plastic bag and then open it on the day as if it was a surprise, pretending to myself that I couldn't remember what it was. It was a ritual I would be repeating a great many times in the coming years. It's a habit I still haven't broken, even after all this time. It drives my wife mad when I buy myself something I want just a few days before my birthday, not thinking that she might have had the same idea.

Another of the early jobs I did was being a milk boy. I would wake myself up at four or five in the morning, while the rest of the family was still asleep, and I'd quietly get dressed, creep downstairs and let myself out of the house. Even though I never had a watch I always knew roughly what the time was and waking up has never been a problem for me. I liked the quiet of the early mornings and the freshness of the air. I would then run around the streets looking for milk floats, listening out for the distinctive hum of their electric engines and the rattle of the bottles in their crates, so that I could offer to help the milkmen with their deliveries. If I managed to find one they nearly always agreed, and paid me for my trouble, but it wasn't always possible to hunt them down in time. Some mornings I'd spend an hour or two searching the streets, until it was too late, and then I'd have to return home empty-handed and already hungry in order not to be late for school. The milkman I liked best sometimes used to pay me with food he carried on the float, rather than money, which I was always happy about because it gave us something for breakfast, which would mean we could get through the morning until lunchtime with full stomachs.

There was an open-air market every Friday in New Addington, filling the car park between the main road and the shops with stalls and vans selling everything you can imagine from wonderful fruit and vegetables to cheap clothes and electronic gadgets. There was a meat auctioneer who would turn up in a huge lorry, let down the side and set up shop right there. I would sit and watch in awe as the men up in the lorry, behind the counter, worked the crowd, shouting out their wares, taking bids, exchanging jokes. Everyone who worked the market seemed to have ready money and to be enjoying what they were doing. I loved the buzz of a world where you lived by the deals you made that day, and the crush of shoppers and browsers as they meandered their way through the tightly packed stalls.

I used to get up early and walk the mile or two up to the precinct to get there as they were arriving in their vans, to offer my services. There was a guy with a toy stall who would give me a couple of pounds to help him set up and lay everything out, which I loved doing. The market would be there in all weathers and I can remember doing it in the snow one year. I only had plimsolls and my feet were so cold I thought they were going to drop off. The full-time workers in the market all had padded moon boots, which were the fashion in the early eighties, and I really wanted a pair of those, but there was no way I could afford them, not even the pairs they sold cheaply in the market. All the money I made had to go on food before it went on keeping my feet warm, so I just had to keep quiet, stamp my feet to keep the blood circulating and get on with it.

In the summer holidays the funfair would come to town and Wayne and I would both go up to help them set up. We would go from stall to stall asking if anyone had any jobs they wanted doing. It was hard physical work. Earning the money was great, but being out of the house and amongst friendly, happy people was the real treat. A few years later my little brother, Robert, ran off with the funfair, just to get away from the torments of home. I think he suffered pretty much the same treatment as I did and the world of the fairground offered him a way to disappear.

When I was eleven I moved to another school. I'd been looking forward to moving from Wolsey Junior, thinking it would give me a fresh start and that I'd be able to make friends at last and be like everyone else. I forgot that all the same children would be moving with me, so nothing would actually change. Even though we were not right behind our house any more, people still knew about my mother and about my nicknames and the stealing and the tempers. It wasn't a nice school. I always found that when other children were on their own they'd talk to me and be quite friendly and normal. As soon as they were in a group, however, they'd ignore me, or hurl insults. It was as if they believed they'd be tainted if they were seen associating with me, as if they might catch my unpopularity and be forced to be outcasts along with me. I could understand why they felt that but it still hurt, and I couldn't see how I could break the cycle of exclusion and unpopularity.

There was one particular girl who'd been quite nice to

me on a number of occasions. One morning, as I was coming in late in a bit of a hurry, I passed her as she was waving through a window to her friends inside the classroom. At just the same moment two boys came out of the building, called me a name and pushed me. I fell against the girl, knocking her into the window and banging her head. I was horrified because I could see she'd hurt herself quite badly and the other two boys had disappeared, leaving me looking like the guilty party. The girl was crying so hard no one asked her for her opinion of what had happened. Because of my history it was immediately assumed I had attacked her and I was dragged in front of the headmaster, who had a reputation for being a cruel man. I tried to explain what had happened but he wouldn't listen. Nobody believed I'd been pushed; they were all convinced I'd just shoved her into the glass for no reason. Why would I do that? I thought to myself as they went on and on at me. She was always nice to me. Why would I attack one of the few people who showed me friendship? Any protests I made were brushed aside, so I fell silent, horribly aware that there was nothing I could do to change their perception of me.

The two guys who had pushed me were also friends with all the other kids who'd witnessed the scene through the window, so no one from in there was going to speak up on my behalf against them, even though they'd seen exactly what had happened.

The headmaster liked to give the impression he was a stern disciplinarian and made it clear that he intended to cane me for this offence.

'But I'm not going to do it immediately because I need to get permission from your parents,' he said. 'I want you to spend a little time thinking about what you've done and about what's going to happen to you.'

'Please don't phone my mother,' I pleaded, knowing that this would give her one more excuse to lay into me herself once I got home, but he was adamant. I guess it was a legal requirement.

And so I had to wait outside the headmaster's office until he was ready to cane me. Getting permission from Gloria, of course, was no more than a formality. Beating me was an activity she thoroughly approved of, whether she did it herself or delegated it to Dennis or anyone else, so I knew there wouldn't be any salvation coming from that quarter. Waiting for pain, when you know it's coming, makes it a hundred times more frightening.

When it was finally time for me to go back in and hold my hand out he didn't spare me at all. It was not enough for him simply to bring the cane down on my outstretched palm. In order to exert maximum force he pulled up a chair and climbed on to it, jumping off each time he brought the cane down on my hand. The pain was incredible and I wasn't able to hide it. I yelled fit to burst as each of the four strokes descended and he climbed back on to the chair again for the next. By that time I was quite seriously malnourished from the appalling diet I was living on, and I was developing anaemia, although I didn't know it, which meant that my resistance to pain was lower than it should have been. My screams could be heard in all the classrooms that lined the corridor up to the headmaster's office.

I was completely unable to hide the tears, even after the caning had finished, because the pain continued to pulse through my hand, making me feel faint and sick as I slowly made my way back to the classroom. Every pair of eyes turned to stare at me as I opened the door and walked in. They all knew what had happened with the girl because they'd witnessed it through the window, and they'd all heard my screams. For the first time ever I thought I saw guilt in some of their faces. It was as if they were beginning to grow up and realize that the way they were treating me was wrong. All of them knew that it had been within their power to speak up and save me from the beating, but none of them had had the courage to do it. I guess that didn't make them feel proud of themselves.

I didn't say anything, just sat down and tried to catch up with whatever was happening in the class. They were all writing something so I picked up my pen, but I wasn't able to hold it because my hand was burning so fiercely and I couldn't think straight because my mind was in such turmoil.

Soon after that incident we were moved to another council house a few miles away in Norbury. I think our neighbours in the Horseshoe had been complaining about the trouble Gloria was always causing and so the council decided to give us a fresh start. Our standard of living didn't improve as a result, and the house, although it was built of bricks rather than tin, was no nicer than the wreck we had left behind us. I did now have a room of my own, but it was the smallest room in the house, designed to be a box room, I would imagine, rather than a bedroom. As far as I was concerned it was just another undecorated and unlit cell. There was one small square window, which allowed the moon to shine through and give me some light to find my way around at night.

Wayne and I were moved to a new school in Mitcham,

which I felt hopeful about, seeing it as a chance to make a new start amongst people who knew nothing of our history. But it wasn't long before our new classmates realized the sort of family we came from and we were excluded socially once more. Wayne went to the new school first and had already started to play truant each day by the time I arrived. I could see the attraction of staying away; at least it freed us from the taunts and the disdainful looks, so we would go off together. Gloria always claimed it was my bad influence that led Wayne astray, which gave her another reason to lay into me at home. But she knew he'd been doing it before, and he carried on after I'd been moved to another school.

Sometimes Wayne and I got on really well and sometimes we loathed each other, like most brothers, I guess. Because he got more new clothes from council clothing grants than I did, being the older one, he tended to be less conspicuous at school. So he hated it when I was around because he got stuck with the same 'tramp' label as me. When he was on his own he could sometimes win people over.

To separate us off I was moved a few months later to Ingram High School for Boys in Norbury, in the hope that I would do better away from Wayne's influence. This was a much nicer school and it was there that I met a teacher called Colin Smith. He seemed to look at me differently to other teachers. He was a tough disciplinarian, a teacher of the old school. He was an immaculate man in everything he did; very firm and no one ever mucked about in his classes, but he was also very fair, and he seemed to think there was something worthwhile about me.

The beatings and jibes were still going on at home and no one at school took any interest in the bruises I was always covered in. Now I was getting older perhaps they assumed they were just the result of normal boyish rough and tumble, but I noticed Colin Smith looking at them when I was in my P.E. kit one day. He asked me about them and I made the usual excuses about falling over and bumping into things. He didn't say anything, just nodded thoughtfully, and I could tell he didn't believe me. I hoped he wouldn't follow it up. I dreaded anyone going round to the house and saying anything, because I knew it would lead to me getting a worse beating once they'd gone. I was also keen that no one at the school got to see how we lived.

Because of the start I'd got at Baldwin's Hill in East Grinstead, I'd managed to stay in the third highest class when I went to secondary school even with my gradually slipping standards. But now, as the pressure was being put on academically, I was finding it hard to keep up, because I still couldn't do homework in the same way as the other children and there was more and more emphasis being put on the work done at home. When there is nowhere to sit, and there is constant shouting and fighting going on all around, it's impossible to concentrate on anything. I couldn't even retreat into my bedroom to work because there was no light once the sun had gone down. Before long I had slipped all the way down to the bottom class.

I was receiving a council token each day to pay for lunch at school, while other children had packed lunches. Although it marked me out as different, I was still very grateful for it. Had it not been for that free meal my health would have deteriorated even more quickly than it did. We still rarely had any breakfast at home and there were chips for supper every single night.

Colin Smith asked me to stay behind after lessons one

day. I went to his office, wondering what I might be in trouble for now.

'How's life at home, Kevin?' he asked, as blunt and to the point as always.

'Fine,' I lied, not able to look him in the eye.

'If there are any problems you can always come and talk to me, you know,' he said.

'Yes, sir,' I said, and beat a hasty retreat.

It was a kind thing for him to say, but I didn't think I would ever have the nerve to actually tell anyone outside the family what went on at home. In fact, things had been getting worse, although at least now I was able to get out of the house for several hours at weekends in order to work.

In my early morning searches I'd met a milkman called John. He was a young guy and I thought he was great. He told me he was a jazz funker and that when he was off work he would wear the hat and the Farrers that were all the rage at the time; driving a squared off Cortina when he wasn't on the milk float. He was exactly the sort of man I wanted to be. He told me his full name was 'A Hundred Per Cent John, because there are so many Johns working in this area'. I worked with him on Friday and Saturday mornings because they were his busiest days, when he had to collect the money from his customers as well as make deliveries.

I enjoyed the work, even though it was hard in the winter because the cold glass of the bottles would stick to your hands and you couldn't wear gloves or the bottles would slip out. I was always trying to find those fingerless gloves that old people wear. I liked the feeling of being useful and of being rewarded fairly for my labours.

John noticed the bruises on me from time to time, just as Colin Smith had, and would sometimes ask me about them. I always had an excuse ready, but I could see he didn't believe me any more than the teacher did. At the end of the round he'd always take me for breakfast at a café opposite the police station and I would have a giant fry up, or even a spaghetti Bolognese if it was nearer lunchtime. The people working in there got to know me and would always give me a bowl so huge even I couldn't finish it. I guess they could see I needed feeding up. By the time they'd finished with me I could hardly move. It was great.

One day during the summer holidays I turned up at John's milk float with a huge bruise around my eye. John didn't say anything; he just looked at it and stayed silent when I offered my usual unconvincing explanation. When we'd finished the round and had had something to eat he told me to hop into his car.

'I'll take you home,' he said. 'I want to have a word with your dad.'

I sat in terrified silence as we made our way back to the house. John was a strong lad and I could see he was spoiling for a fight. I dreaded to think what would happen once he'd gone and I was left to their mercy. He didn't say anything either. He seemed to be seething with anger.

'Please,' I said eventually, as he turned into our road, 'just leave it.' But he still didn't reply.

There was a concrete path from the pavement through the open, debris-strewn front garden. Sometimes that path felt like the longest walk in the world. I could see John glancing at the chaos all around and averting his eyes so as not to embarrass me. He knocked loudly on the door as I stood beside him on the step, trembling. We could hear raised voices inside.

Eventually Dennis opened the door and I breathed a sigh

of relief that it wasn't Gloria. The two of them stood looking at one another. Neither of them said anything. I guess John thought he'd made his point just by being there for me. Without so much as a nod or a smile he turned and walked back to his car. I went into the house. Dennis closed the door behind me and said I wasn't to work for John any more. He must have known exactly what message John was conveying with that meaningful silence. I never saw A Hundred Per Cent John again.

As well as working as a milk boy in the early mornings, I would team up with Wayne and try anything to make extra money in the evenings, weekends and holidays. We didn't mind how many hours we put in because it always meant we were out of the house and earning money for food. We'd do 'penny for the guy' in October and in December we'd go carol singing. We were terrible singers. On Christmas Eve one year we were doing our rounds and were working some houses on a busy roundabout. I doubt if anyone inside the houses could hear us over the traffic noise, but we were giving it our best shot. In a moment of high spirits I put my foot on a wall outside one of the houses we were singing at. The wall collapsed beneath me and we ran for our lives.

We were still laughing about it a few minutes later as we walked past a church. From inside we could hear people singing carols. They were doing it properly, not like us, and it was a very attractive sound. Neither of us had ever been inside a church before and our curiosity got the better of us. We crept up to the door, summoning up all our courage. It had a huge iron handle, which I turned cautiously. I pushed open the door and peered through at the dimly lit interior. We stared up in amazement at the tall ceilings, which stretched above the small congregation. Flickering candles lit the scene and a rich musty scent of age and polish filled my nostrils. The singing came to an end just as we looked in and I dropped the door handle, sending a mighty clang echoing round the quiet building.

The vicar looked up and saw us, frozen in embarrassment on the threshold, and smiled welcomingly, gesturing for us to come in. We obeyed, curious to see what was going on and comforted by the atmosphere of the place, and sat down in an empty pew at the back, listening attentively as they went back to their singing. As we sat there, in that beautiful place, Wayne and I exchanged looks and we both knew at the same moment that we loved each other. No matter what we'd been through in our short lives, or how much we resented one another from time to time, we knew that much. We didn't stay long, the moment was never repeated and neither of us ever mentioned it, but I've never forgotten it.

Christmas came and went as usual. While other children wanted it to last as long as possible so they could be with their friends and families, giving and receiving presents and enjoying big meals, Wayne and I just wanted it to be over so we could go back out looking for new work. It was beyond any of our capabilities to generate a festive spirit in a house so steeped in hatred and misery.

A local newsagent in Thornton Heath high street said we could do a newspaper round for him if we wanted, but said we'd have to be at the shop by five in the morning. The next morning we were there, dead on five, having walked all the way from the house, but he didn't turn up till after seven. He didn't offer any explanation or apology. It seemed an unnecessarily cruel and inconsiderate gesture, but we weren't in a position to complain because we wanted the work and knew that if we didn't do as he said he'd have no trouble finding other kids who would. He must have been able to tell how desperate we were for money and he offered us other jobs around his house, cleaning up leaves, walking his Dobermann (or should I say allowing the Dobermann to take us for walks), or whatever needed doing. Even though we didn't like the man we were grateful for any chances to earn.

Wayne had managed to get a couple of second-hand fishing rods and, because it was him, Gloria hadn't made a fuss about bringing them into the house. If they'd been mine she would have beaten me with them until they snapped. Sometimes the newsagent would pay us with drink and crisps instead of cash, which we'd take with us and go fishing in a nearby pond. Occasionally we'd use the free train passes we got because of Dennis having worked for British Rail and travel down to Brighton to fish in the sea. They were always great days out. We never caught anything and we wouldn't have had a clue what to do if we had, but it made me feel, at least for a few hours, like we were Tom Sawyer and Huck Finn on an adventure. I loved the feeling of freedom when we came out of Brighton station and I could smell the sea air and knew that we could please ourselves for the whole day. Even though we didn't have any money to do anything on the pier or in any of the amusement arcades or snack bars, we could still use the beach and watch the waves and the other holidaymakers. It gave us a chance to empty our minds and dream a little of what life could be like once we were finally free of our parents. It felt a long walk back up the hill to the station when we knew we were on our way home again.

I was also cleaning cars on Sundays on my own. From

nine o'clock in the morning I would walk to a nearby street and be knocking on doors with my bucket, sponge and Fairy Liquid, offering my services around the neighbourhood. I'd work right through the day, ignoring the traffic that passed a few inches from my back as I lathered and rinsed and rubbed the parked cars with every ounce of energy I could muster. I built up a number of regular customers who I would do first, before going in search of new business. Although I didn't realize it, my health was beginning to seriously deteriorate due to the way we lived, which meant that by the end of the day I was completely shattered. But I enjoyed the work and the freedom that the money was starting to give me.

One of the houses I knocked at was occupied by two men. It was a Victorian semi in a row of identical houses. I cleaned their car every week and they were always very pleasant, giving me a biscuit and a glass of milk while I worked. The house had a black door, which I would come to early on in my round. One Sunday morning I was chatting to one of the men while I was collecting my money, having finished their car, and he asked if I did any other work.

'I might do,' I shrugged, quite willing to try anything that would earn money, even though I was still only twelve years old.

It was summer time and I noticed he was wearing shorts as he led me down the side of the house and through the back garden to a shed. I wondered if he wanted me to do some gardening, or clear out the shed. I didn't mind what it was as long as he paid me.

'Do you like young men?' he asked once we were inside the shed and he had carefully closed the door behind us.

He might as well have asked me if I liked green Martians.

I didn't have a clue what he was on about, but a feeling of disquiet was stirring in my stomach. Something about this scene didn't seem quite right. It didn't seem to be the sort of question he should be asking. I don't think I said anything, although I may have made some sort of non-committal noise out of politeness. Whatever my response was, he obviously took it as encouragement. He rummaged around in a drawer and pulled out a magazine, indicating that I should have a look at it. I did as I was told and the stirrings of disquiet in my stomach tightened into pangs of panic. The pages were covered in glossy pictures of naked men in sexually provocative poses. I didn't know where to look. I felt scared and sick and wanted to run away, but I had to stay because he hadn't paid me my money.

'Do you like that?' he asked, pointing to one of the pictures and my stomach did a somersault.

I said nothing, my throat having closed down and my brain gone numb. I realized he was holding my hand and I froze, not knowing what to do or say, trying to think how to snatch it away from him without offending him and losing my car-washing money. I felt him guiding my hand towards his shorts and realized they were undone and he was wearing nothing underneath. I was suddenly galvanized into action, pulling my hand out of his grip. Now that I'd finally reacted he must have realized he'd made a mistake because he stepped back and apologized. I left as fast as I could, grabbing the money that he held out to me and running back down the garden and out past the house into the safety of the busy road outside.

There was a park across the road, which I ran over to and sat down on a bench, trying to compose my thoughts and calm my thumping heart. I felt furious because now I was frightened to continue with the cleaning round, and it had been the first thing I'd ever done that made me feel totally free and independent of anyone else. It seemed there wasn't anything I could do, or anywhere I could go where other people wouldn't interfere with me in some way. At home I had the beatings and the taunting, at school there were the jibes and now someone else had tainted my work. Even though I was out of the house and out of the school and earning money, I still wasn't free.

As I sat there, gathering my thoughts, I grew determined not to let one man mess up the best day of my week and so, once I'd recovered from the shock, I continued working, attacking the cars with twice the usual vigour, my strength fuelled by my anger. I ended up earning £13 that day, more than I ever had before. I continued building the round in the coming weeks, but from then on I went past the black front door at the speed of light, and I never told a single soul about what had happened in that shed. When I got home Gloria took the money off me, promising to pay me back when the Giro came through, but I never saw it again.

12

It Has to Get Worse Before It Can Get Better

I knew Colin Smith, my teacher, had worked out what was happening to me at home. I could feel his eyes resting on whatever new bruise or mark I was unable to hide whenever I went into school. He would occasionally ask me about them, but he was always willing to drop the subject when I made it obvious I didn't want to talk about it. I could tell he didn't believe my stories, but I couldn't find a way to tell him the truth.

The social services were still visiting us, but their calls were becoming less and less regular and Gloria was always able to cover up whatever was wrong with me on the day they showed up. By this time I wasn't just taking whatever beatings were doled out to me. I was defending myself; kicking and punching back with all my strength. It made things worse because it fuelled her temper, but I had to do something, I couldn't just lie there and accept whatever she wanted to do to me. It seems incredible now to think that I had to physically fight my own mother in order to defend myself, but at the time it just seemed like part of my normal life.

One morning, when I arrived at school late, I was particularly badly shaken by whatever had happened at home before I came out and it must have been obvious to anyone who looked at me that something was wrong. Colin called me into his office.

'Are you being hit at home?' he asked, bluntly.

'Yes,' I replied, no longer feeling able to lie to him. I was reaching the end of my tether. I was almost ready to stand up to my tormentors once and for all.

He must have passed the information on to social services but, as usual, they didn't get to the house for a few days, by which time my bruises had faded again.

They must have been suspicious and wanted to talk to me away from the noise and interference of the rest of the family because eventually a male social worker arrived at the school and questioned me there. I thought that maybe this time they would realize their mistake in returning me home and I would be able to get back to Yarborough, but at the same time I was wary. I didn't want to say too much about what Gloria did, in case they didn't take me away immediately and I had to face her on my own with her knowing that I'd betrayed her.

At the end of the school day the man came home with me to talk to Gloria and Dennis. I was absolutely terrified; imagining how mad Gloria was going to go the moment the social worker had gone. Dennis was there, as silent and sheepish as always, and the man faced both of them, telling them that the social services were thinking of taking me into emergency care. To my horror I could see Dennis was near to tears and Gloria started pleading with me not to go, promising that things would get better. I just wanted to turn round and walk out of the house with the social worker, but I could see that he was wavering, unsure what to do in the face of such emotion.

'All right, Kevin,' he said eventually. 'Tell us what you would like to do. Do you want to stay here with your family, or would you like us to take you into care?'

My heart sank. How could I say, in front of my weeping father and pleading mother, that I wanted to be taken into care? What if the social worker didn't take me immediately, what sort of revenge would Gloria wreak on me the moment the door closed behind our visitor? And in the back of my mind a nagging voice was saying perhaps things would get better now that there had been a warning, maybe she really would make an effort.

Unable to say what I really felt and betray my parents so totally, I mumbled that I wanted to stay at home. The trap had sprung shut on me. The social worker had put me into a position where I had no choice but to seal my own fate. Not only did my parents now think I was shopping them to the authorities; the authorities thought I was messing them about and didn't want to be helped. I felt completely desolate.

Colin Smith wasn't fooled when I told him what had happened the next day. He could see the man had put me in an impossible position. Although I didn't know anything about it at the time, I think I must have been put on a list somewhere as a potentially endangered child, and he was watching my every move at school, ready to report anything suspicious.

The warning had had no effect on Gloria or Dennis and they forgot their emotional appeal almost immediately the man walked out the door. The fighting was getting worse and worse as they got increasingly on each other's nerves. One day they were coming to blows upstairs in the girls' bedroom. As with other fights that I'd witnessed between them they weren't holding anything back, both of them punching and kicking as they screamed foul-mouthed abuse at one another. We were all shouting at them from outside the room to stop and the girls were in tears. It looked as if someone was going to end up being killed.

At that moment something inside my head snapped. I started to scream, so loudly that I was no longer able to hear myself. It was as if I'd gone beyond hearing anything that was happening either around me or inside my own head. It felt as if I'd stepped out of my body. I'd had enough of this life. I just wanted it to stop. Despite all the noise the others were making, this terrible wail silenced them. Both the grown-ups stopped, mid-punch, and stared in amazement at me as I stood there with my mouth wide open and this fearful sound howling out, as if I'd just had thousands of volts shot through me. People must have been able to hear me from several streets away.

The next thing I knew I'd been knocked to the floor and Gloria was dragging me into the room with them. Both of them left the other one alone, all the grievances that had caused the fight in the first place apparently forgotten, and they started laying into me with more force than they ever had before. It was the worst beating I'd ever had and it kept on going. Their anger seemed to give them superhuman powers and they kept punching and kicking and slapping me. The other children were going wild with panic, thinking their brother was going to be killed in front of their eyes.

'Leave him alone!' I heard them shriek. 'Leave him alone!' Some of them received passing smacks for their interference if they tried to venture into the room to rescue me. Both the grown-ups were lost in a frenzy of violence.

Eventually, after what seemed like an eternity, they seemed to wear themselves out and I felt the strength ebbing from their blows. Dennis gave up first, going off downstairs, puffing, physically unable to do any more, while Gloria continued biting me with whatever strength she had left. Finally she too ground to a halt, panting and exhausted. In the stillness that followed the storm she must have realized she'd gone too far, that this time she just might be unable to hide the damage she'd done to me. She left the room while I was curled up on the bed, unable to move.

Some moments later she came back in. With an awkward shift in mood she put her arm round me. It was the first time I'd ever known her to show me any affection at all, either physical or emotional, and it felt very strange. Perhaps she hoped she could cajole me into staying silent for a little longer, knowing she'd gone too far and might this time be found out. Strains of Elvis came up from the kitchen. I left my arms at my side, not wanting to touch her. The next day I heard her boasting to the whole neighbourhood how Kevin had gone up to her and cuddled her. She never held me again, and I certainly never held her.

The next morning I was still in terrible pain but dragged myself out of bed, not wanting to be trapped in the house with her any longer. It was hard to stand up. I was covered in marks and bruises. I had over twenty bite marks on my neck, shoulders and arms where Gloria had bitten down with her gums, using all her strength. If she'd had her teeth in she would have ripped my throat out with the power of those bites. There was no way I could cover all these up. They looked like love bites, which meant the other boys at school noticed them immediately.

'Lewis's been kissed by Dracula,' one shouted and the others caught on, repeating the mantra and repeating it, over and over again. This was an all-boys school; a boy covered in hickeys wasn't going to be shown any mercy.

Getting myself from the house to the playground had

taken all my energy and once I was there my legs gave out underneath me. I collapsed on to the tarmac and dissolved into tears. I didn't feel I could go on any longer. One of the teachers came over and picked me up, seeing that I winced in pain as she touched me. I was taken into the nurse's room and Colin Smith came in to take a look at me. I could see he was shocked by what he saw and he went away to call social services. But when he spoke to them they told him I'd expressed a wish to stay in the family home and they were reluctant to interfere with my decision. I knew I wanted to go, but only if they would take me away immediately. I didn't want Gloria to know I was going but still have access to me, even if it was only for a few days.

Colin must have protested and insisted that the social worker came to look at me again. But he didn't come round to the house again for a couple of weeks, by which time the marks had faded once more. The social services must then have reported this back to Colin because he took me into his office again the following day.

'I'm sorry, Kevin,' he said, and I could see from his face that he meant it. 'I'm afraid it has to get worse before it gets better.'

I could tell he was choked up at having to give me the news. I don't think he could quite believe they were going to allow me to go back home for more of the same, but he'd obviously discovered he couldn't do anything about it. He'd done everything he could and nothing was going to change. The news didn't shock me as much as it did him. I'd come to expect nothing from social services, because it was them that had delivered me back to Gloria from Yarborough and they didn't seem to have done anything to help me since then.

Even though I was still weak for my age, I was now getting bigger. I was starting to learn how to defend myself better from the blows, trying to kick her away. Sometimes I'd be in my bedroom on my own and I'd hear her thumping up the stairs, swearing and screaming abuse back down at Dennis, and I'd know she was heading for me. I would prepare myself to fight back as hard as I could, hunching myself into a ball to protect myself. But by doing that I was increasing her anger and she was still much stronger and much more vicious than me, so the punishment I received was far worse than it had been when I had put up no struggle. I was also trying harder and harder not to cry now that I was growing up, and that seemed to make her all the more determined to keep going until she'd managed to draw tears from me.

I felt totally alone. I was still excluded by the other kids at school and even my brothers and sisters tended to avoid me in case they got a smack from Gloria for associating with me.

My smallest brother, Robert, was now six or seven years old, and she seemed to have taken as great a dislike to him as she had to me. She'd pick on him in just the same way, hitting him and taunting him. In an attempt to escape from the house Robert had befriended an old man who lived nearby and worked for the council. The man used to take Robert to the swings a lot, giving him a break from the house and from Gloria's bullying. Sometimes Robert would even stay over for the night at this man's house. On one occasion I was invited to go round with him. It was a much more comfortable house than ours and there were enough bedrooms for us to have one each so I was perfectly happy with the arrangement. It was like a little holiday.

I'd gone to bed already, enjoying the smell and feel of the clean bedclothes, when I heard noises coming from Robert's room next door. I thought I should check he was all right and went in without announcing myself. The two of them were sitting side by side on the bed and Robert had his pyjama trousers down around his knees. I felt a chill of fear run through me, as I had with the man in the shed on the car-washing round.

'Leave him alone,' I said, feeling deeply protective of my little brother, in a way that no one in the family had ever felt about me.

The man jumped up and I could see he was worried. At the time I didn't have any idea just how much trouble he would be in if I told on him, but he must have known. Once I was sure Robert was safely tucked up in bed I went back to my own room, but I didn't sleep well that night, half listening for any suspicious movements on the landing outside. The next morning the man took us both out to the shops and gave us every treat imaginable before taking us home.

I thought about the scene I'd witnessed a great deal and decided I had to do something, if only to protect other children who might be lured into his house. I couldn't trust Gloria or Dennis to protect Robert from this man, so I would have to do it myself. When we next got a visit from a social worker there was the usual uproar of everyone trying to have their say at once, but I eventually managed to catch his attention and told him what I'd seen. He seemed to be listening, but nothing ever happened. I don't think he believed me, or if he did they must have thought my evidence would never stand up in court. A few years later

Robert's friend was arrested for an offence against some other child. If they'd only believed me they could have spared that child, and maybe others in between, from all that trauma. But I suppose there was just too much going on in our house for them to be able to act on everything. It must have been like walking over the threshold into hell for them every time they passed our front door. They certainly acted as if we were some alien and slightly frightening species and, I guess, from their point of view, we were. It never felt as if they believed anything we told them, and they gave off an air of arrogance, as if they always knew better than us. I suppose they did know better about most things, but I never felt confident they would help me, even if I asked them directly.

From time to time I'd play with other children in the street. There was one boy, Errol, who I befriended for a while and we used to play together on a local cricket field just across the road. One evening, after school, we went up there with his younger sister. We were playing around the pavilion when we saw two dogs mating. Errol and I were probably sniggering, like small boys do at such things, but his sister went over to pet the dogs. Obviously they didn't want to be disturbed and one of them went for her. She turned and ran, her face contorted with fear, as the dog snapped and snarled at her heels. It managed to get her dress in its teeth and ripped the material. I grabbed a stick and a stone and chased the animal without a second thought. I felt no fear whatsoever. I went after the dog to protect the small child. I threw the stone first, missing the dog but giving it enough of a fright to make it run off in the opposite direction.

The Kid

It didn't seem like anything special at the time, just a natural reaction. I felt proud of myself for that. One day I knew I was going to be brave enough to stand up to Gloria once and for all.

13

New Horizons

Colin Smith must have been more worried about me during that time than he let on; perhaps he was afraid he'd made things worse by interfering, that he shouldn't have stirred up trouble that would rebound on me. Although he was so kind to me personally, he never showed me any favouritism inside the school. Quite rightly, I had to behave just like everyone else. He was always totally fair like that, but outside the classroom he did the most amazing thing, something completely unexpected that opened up a whole new world for me. I guess that's the definition of what a good teacher should be able to do for his pupils.

He called me into his office at the end of a school day and said he had something that he thought I would like. He then gave me a Walkman personal stereo and a tape of popular classical songs that he'd made for me in his own time. At first I was simply touched to receive any sort of present at all. If nobody ever gives you anything it really is the 'thought that counts' when they do. I was puzzled as to why he'd think to give me a Walkman, but was intrigued by the idea of trying out something new. Although it was a second-hand machine it was probably the most generous gift anyone had ever given me, and the fact that he'd gone to the trouble to make a recording just for me of something he thought I would like made it priceless.

My immediate problem, as with anything I managed to acquire, was how to get it into the house without Gloria spotting it and taking it away or smashing it out of sheer spite. I hatched a plan to smuggle it past her in my pants, the bulge carefully concealed by my blazer until I got upstairs to my poky little bedroom. My heart was pounding as I came into the door, trying to look natural as I picked my way through the debris that always greeted anyone who stepped through the door. I didn't say a word, or even look in her direction. The worst thing that could happen would be for me to draw attention to myself and annoy her, because if she started hitting me she would either discover the stereo, or smash it with one of her blows. Out of the corner of my eye I could see her giving me a look, like a vicious old guard dog too lazy to raise its head when someone passes by, and I kept walking. I reached the stairs, which were just as covered in junk as the hallway, and made my way up, forcing myself not to go too fast, not to look suspicious, not to attract her attention in any way. Once I was safely in the bedroom I could breathe again, and remove my prize from its sweaty hiding place.

Since virtually every possession I'd ever had had either been taken from me or destroyed, I was always meticulous in my security precautions with anything I did smuggle into the house. I'd developed a habit of hiding the few possessions I'd managed to acquire inside the mattress of my bed. I knew they were safe there because Gloria never changed the sheets, so I'd made a slit in the mattress and I now pushed my worldly possessions, including the Walkman, inside. The stained, worn mattress became its home. I would even leave it in there while it was playing, so that only the headphones would have to be hidden if someone came in unexpectedly. From then on a large percentage of my earnings had to be set aside each week to buy batteries, so that I never ran out.

I'd never stopped to really listen to music before and Colin Smith's tape was a revelation. I would lie in bed at night with the headphones on, lost in the classical music, letting my mind wander as far as possible from the reality of my surroundings. It was so peaceful, as if the orchestra was serenading me on my way to America. The first time I listened a song came up called 'Ebben? Ne andrò lontana'. To begin with it scared me but as I played it more and more it grew on me. It soon became my favourite; so tranquil and eloquent, as if the mummer was singing just to me, sending me to sleep each night.

I could never tell anyone else about my growing passion for classical music because they'd think I was weird to be listening to it at my age. I had enough of a reputation for being different without letting people know I had 'nerdy' tastes in music as well. So for a long time I would only use it to go to sleep at night, my head full of images of escaping to America as I let it roll over me. Even in those limited doses, the music was changing my life. It felt as if until that moment I'd been trapped in a cupboard with no doors, and suddenly a door had opened. At the same time it was frustrating because although the door was open, showing me a view of another world, I was still sitting inside the cupboard and unable to step outside. My love for music increased with every waking moment. As I became braver, I would smuggle the Walkman out of the house and sit in the park to listen to the music in the fresh air, surrounded by greenery. I was able to get into a new world that was mine and mine alone. For the first time I'd discovered something that allowed my mind to rest. I could finally understand why my father had wanted to spend all those hours in the kitchen listening to Elvis, how it would have soothed his soul after all the shouting and ugliness and given his exhausted mind a chance to escape from the ugliness into something else.

The best thing was when I went to visit Gini and Guy, because I could smuggle the stereo out in my pants when Gini came to collect me: Gloria would never hit me or question me in front of her. Guy would then lend me his tapes, which I would play all day long until it was time to go back into the house, when the Walkman had to go back into its hiding place. I never took my own tape with me in case Guy took the mickey out of me for liking something so strange. I was just as happy listening to the sort of pop music most people our age were into. On Sunday evenings Gini wouldn't take me home until Guy and I finished listening to the top forty charts on Radio 1, taping the whole chart so that we could listen to it again next time I came. I used to get a sinking feeling in my stomach as the programme moved further and further up the charts because I knew the moment of my return home was getting closer. The number-one record, which should have been the high point of the programme, was actually the moment when I knew my day out was over and it was time to get into the car and start the sad journey home to Norbury.

I had managed to acquire one or two other possessions, with extreme stealth. Something I'd always wanted, but knew I'd never get, was a train set. One evening I was passing a parish hall after doing some job or other and had a little money in my pocket. I saw a sign advertising a jumble sale and popped inside. The hall was full of trestle tables, all covered in old clothes and bits and bobs, and surrounded by larger items such as worn-out ironing boards and old-fashioned electric fires. As I joined the crowds, rummaging through the piles of junk in the hope of finding something I could afford with the pennies left over from my earnings, I came across a few pieces of an old train set, all bound together with an elastic band. I think it was priced at something like a pound, which I could just afford. I bought it, almost beside myself with excitement at finally owning my own train set. Once again the problem then was getting it into the house without being spotted, since it was too big to fit into my underpants without doing me a serious injury.

So I decided not to take a big risk and to wait for my opportunity. If I was caught with it I'd not only lose the train, I would also be beaten for my temerity in thinking I could own something the others didn't have. As I walked back from the hall my mind was racing as I clutched my booty under my jumper. When I got to the house I crept round the side into the garden, careful to make sure no one saw me through the windows. I found something sharp enough to dig a hole and buried my treasure. I then waited until a few days later, when Gloria went out to cash her Giro and I knew she would be out of the house for at least an hour, before digging it up. I dusted the earth off and hurried up to my bedroom with it, sliding it into the mattress, padding it carefully with the stuffing to make sure it wouldn't make a noise and give me away if, by some remote chance, Gloria decided to do something with the beds. Then I loosely stitched up the hole.

I had a needle and a length of cotton, which I used to hold together the rip in the mattress cover each time I put something away. Then, once I was sure Gloria was safely in bed or engrossed in doing something else, I'd open up the stitching, get out the train and set up the few pieces of track for it to run back and forth on, lost in my own imaginary world for a few minutes before I had to pack it all away again. I lived in fear of her finding the needle while I was out at school and working out what it was for. I knew if that happened she wouldn't hesitate to stick it into me in order to make the punishment fit the crime.

One night I'd been playing with my train while listening to my music and I was so tired I didn't bother to sew them back into the mattress. It had been so long since Gloria had been near my room I'd been lulled into a false sense of security. So I just pushed everything out of sight under the bed, meaning to secrete it away the next day. Unfortunately she chose that day to go into my cell while I was at school and she found everything. Perhaps she was suspicious of the amount of time I spent in there on my own, or perhaps she was looking for money and thought I might be hiding some of my earnings from her. When I got home and discovered what had happened I was terrified, certain I would be in for a terrible beating. But she didn't explode immediately, as I thought she would, she just gave all my prized possessions to Wayne, except the tape, which she threw away. She wanted to know where the music had come from and I told her that Colin Smith had given it to me.

She must have been brooding on the situation because that evening she decided I did deserve a beating after all, if only for receiving favouritism from a teacher. She wound herself up into a furious temper, convincing herself I needed to be taught a lesson I wouldn't forget, and came after me late that night, when I was already in my grubby pyjamas, lying on my bed and missing my music. She didn't come up alone. Dennis was dragged out of the kitchen and into the row and he started laying into me in a drunken rage that she kept on stoking up. Perhaps he too was jealous that another adult had shown me some kindness, when no one ever did the same for him. Or perhaps he felt guilty that he wasn't able to give me anything I needed or wanted. Or perhaps he felt nothing at all except anger at being disturbed from his drinking. Whatever was driving him, he just kept on hitting me. I was frightened that things were going to get out of control again so I managed to wriggle free of them both and clattered downstairs. There was confusion at the top of the stairs behind me as they both tried to get after me at once, and in those few seconds I managed to throw open the front door and run out into the street, still in my pyjamas. Once there I couldn't think where to go. I didn't want to loiter in the park opposite the house in the dark, and I didn't have any friends whose houses I could go to. The school was closed and I had no idea where Colin Smith or any of the teachers lived. The only place I could think of going to for help was the local police station on the other side of the park.

I must have cut a sorry little figure as I walked into the police station, barefooted and out of breath, and told them what was happening to me. There were three officers on duty, one woman and two men, and they all seemed to be towering over me, looking down their noses as they told me there was nothing they could do to help because it was all happening in the privacy of my own home.

Exhausted, cold and rejected, I walked back out of the station into the night, padding down the road and into the house again on my own. There was nowhere else for me to go. They wouldn't even escort me home across the dark park. Luckily, by the time I got in, Gloria and Dennis's anger had burned itself out in my absence and I was able to crawl back into bed without catching their attention or rekindling the fight.

Next time I went to visit Gini she wanted to know what had happened to the Walkman, because she knew how much it had meant to me and didn't believe I would just have forgotten it. I told her Gloria had taken it away and that afternoon she took me out into East Grinstead and bought me a new one. I no longer had the tape that Colin Smith had made for me, but at least I had the ones Guy and I had made of the pop charts. I was very touched that Gini would do such a thing for me, and nervous that Gloria would take this one away from me as well. When Gini dropped me off that evening she made a point of telling Gloria she'd bought it for me. Gloria was always trying to be friends with Gini and I knew she wouldn't take this machine if she thought Gini had bought it.

Gloria was always looking for friends she could pour her heart out to, and the more she tried to be friendly the more people recoiled from the force and volume of her bitterness. Whether it was social workers or people like Gini who wanted to help me, she was just too much for them to take. Occasionally, she would tease me by putting the new Walkman up out of my reach, provoking an argument for the sake of it, but she didn't dare take it away from me for good, because then she would have had to explain to Gini why she'd done it.

The beatings were still becoming worse and the scream-ing in my ear was constant, partly because I was getting bigger and trying to defend myself, driving Gloria to ever greater frenzies of violence, partly because the pressures of life were becoming worse for her as we all grew bigger and Dennis slipped further under the influence of drink. She was like a ferocious animal caged in a zoo that couldn't be trusted to co-habit with any others for fear she'd turn on them. She also became careless about where she marked me, not able to control her blows as carefully when I was ducking and diving and fighting back. The bruises and marks on my face and body became impossible to ignore at school and the social services, again at Colin Smith's instigation, couldn't put off taking me away any longer. This time when they came to see me at school and asked if I wanted to leave the family, I said I did. A social worker came home with me to collect my few possessions and to inform Gloria and Dennis what was happening.

My mother only had one question to ask as I was being led down the path to the car. 'Does this mean they'll be stopping his child benefit?'

That summed it all up for me. I guess that was the only reason they'd asked to have me back in the first place.

14

Margaret and Alan

I just couldn't stop saying 'sorry'. It was the word that sprang to my lips at the start of virtually every sentence. I was so used to being wrong, so used to being punished. Apologizing never stopped the punishment, but it had become like a nervous tic. I couldn't stop myself, even when I hadn't done anything wrong. It was an attempt at self-defence, admitting I was wrong from the start so no one would have to beat it out of me.

When they took me away again I'd hoped that social services would return me to Yarborough so that I could take up my life where I'd left off. But no one suggested that and I would never have been presumptuous enough to bring up the subject myself. I didn't feel that I had any power over my own destiny; I just had to do what they told me, go where they put me, and hope for the best. They immediately started talking about fostering me with other families. I was disappointed. I hadn't particularly enjoyed the fostering experience before, always feeling like an outsider in the families I was placed with, knowing I was only there because they were being paid to look after me. But I didn't argue, anything would be better than being at home. I now knew for sure that my parents had only wanted to have me in the house because it brought in more money, so where was the difference?

When the authorities had time to look into my health, once they'd got me out of the house and didn't have to fend off my mother and other members of the family, they diagnosed me as anaemic. It was assumed that it was because of the appalling diet I'd been having for the previous four years, and they were probably right. If you feed people really badly for long enough eventually they will become weak and sick. Everyone agreed that I needed building up, both physically and psychologically. It was now 1984 and I was thirteen years old. I probably wasn't the easiest of children to place. It would take some very special people to be able to handle a teenager who had been damaged as badly as I had by then.

I was told that a temporary family had been found for me in Coulsdon, a few miles away. It looked as if I was going to be shifted around from pillar to post all over again. The couple, they said, were called Margaret and Alan and I was going to be taken round to meet them that evening. The house I was driven to was a nicely kept suburban semi, with bay windows and red tiles on the walls. The road was pleasant and lined with trees, a little like the ones I'd known around Yarborough. It was obviously a good neighbourhood. The moment they opened the door to the social worker's knock I could see Margaret and Alan were the exact opposite of Gloria and Dennis. At the most superficial level they were opposite sizes. Where Gloria had towered over Dennis physically, Alan was a tall, lean man. Where Gloria had been hard and aggressive looking, Margaret was soft, round and maternal. Margaret looked a bit younger than her husband, but I still didn't reckon she was going to be able to hit me as hard as I was used to. I was introduced to them as 'Uncle Alan and Auntie Margaret'.

The house was as well kept inside as out. It smelled clean and everything seemed to be polished and in its proper place. It was a real family home, well used down the years but cherished and cared for. On that first visit, as the social worker chatted to them, Margaret made me a baked potato with baked beans and cheese on top. It was such a simple, basic meal to them, but it was a combination of textures and tastes I'd never experienced before and to me it was the most delicious thing I'd ever had. If you've lived on a diet of chips for four years even a baked potato seems like a feast. I was so hungry and it smelled so good as Margaret served it up, that I stuffed it into my mouth too fast and blistered the roof of my mouth. I quickly swallowed some cold water, anxious not to show myself up.

Alan, I was soon to discover, was a tremendously wise man. He had run his own local business, and was so successful that by the time he retired and sold up, he owned five shops and a distribution business. He was still active in the business world, doing the book-keeping for some of his friends in the trade. Margaret ran the home beautifully, cooked all the meals and helped her husband with the business. They'd worked hard all their lives and they loved children. When their own grew up, they felt there was a gap in their lives, so they decided to take up emergency fostering. It was agreed that I should move in with them for a few months, while the social services worked out what to do with me.

I was very nervous about moving into such a nice house. I was still wetting the bed at that stage, even though I was fourteen years old, and I was still haunted by the nightmares that would make me wake up screaming when everyone else in the house was asleep. I thought it would be embarrassing to show myself up in front of such nice, calm, self-controlled people. But I was so glad to be away from Gloria and Dennis that these seemed like minor worries and I began to believe that maybe I could make a new start. If I was living in a normal home with normal people I would be able to dress like everyone else, and wash like everyone else, and I would be eating the same food and building up my strength. I wouldn't have to look and smell different any more. The change to a proper diet was such a shock to my system that I developed terrible mouth ulcers as a reaction, but they soon faded. I thought I would finally be able to put my 'tramp' image behind me.

I was desperately eager to please them, and Alan and Margaret worked hard to persuade me that I didn't have to say 'sorry' all the time. I kept asking permission for everything, wanting to know what I should be doing, terrified of doing the wrong thing and incurring their displeasure and being sent back home. I had lost all self-confidence. I thought I must be as useless as my mother was always telling me I was.

I was continuing at the same school and Margaret suggested we go out and get me some new bits of uniform to smarten up my appearance. Because they were an older couple, with grown-up children, they were slightly out of touch with the way young people thought and behaved. That would have been all right, I just needed kindness, nurturing and guidance, which they were both more than qualified to help with, but I also needed help in not looking different from everyone else. While we were out Margaret spotted a pair of trousers in a second-hand shop that were ten pence and were the right colour for school. The only problem was they were bell-bottoms, and this was at a time when every other boy was wearing narrow trousers. It sounds like a trivial point, but anyone who can remember being a school child will also remember how perilously a child's reputation can hang on these small points. As long as I was wearing these conspicuously unfashionable trousers, I was still going to be different; and as long as I was different I would continue to be an outsider. These trousers were enormous, but I was far too shy to say anything to Margaret, who was being so kind about buying me new clothes in the first place, and I was terrified of doing anything wrong that might lead to me being sent away from their house. I accepted the hideous trousers without a murmur, but inside I just wanted to shrivel up and die.

Now that I had less to worry about at home, these flares started to occupy an inordinate amount of my thoughts. I had to travel a long way to school on the bus from Coulsdon to Norbury and I would hunch myself into a corner in the hope that no one would be able to see my legs, encased as they were in the huge folds of flapping material. I would try to hide them in class and everywhere around the school, but I was kidding myself – everyone knew I was wearing them.

The other children at school had heard that I'd been taken into care and my nickname changed from 'Tramp' to 'Fosters' or 'Fosters Lager', or sometimes they would call me 'Flares'. So I might have been freed from the violence and the bruises, but I still wasn't free from being different and excluded. People still didn't want to be associated with me, for fear that they would be tarred with the same brush.

At the end of the next term Margaret arranged for me to move to Purley High School for Boys, a more local school in Coulsdon. It was a good school and, more importantly, it was my big chance to shake off my past and start again with a clean slate. All through the summer holidays I had knots in my stomach when I thought about having to meet a whole new set of children, wearing those horrible trousers. A new school seemed like a real chance for me to escape my past, but I knew those flares would ruin my chances of being accepted. The moment I walked through the door in them I would be branded as an outsider.

Just before I went back for the start of term, Margaret and I went out to get me a blazer, and she bought a new pair of trousers as well, normal ones. It was like a giant weight being lifted off my chest. I was suddenly completely normal, from top to bottom. I started the school like any other new boy and was instantly accepted. But Margaret still wanted me to rotate the new trousers with the flares, to get the wear from them. I started secretly making holes in the flares in the hope she'd throw them out, but she was a good housekeeper and sewed the holes up as fast as I could make them. Every weekend I was terrified I'd have to wear the bell-bottoms and when she got my uniform out I would swap them over in secret. I was determined to be a normal child from now on. I treated the new pair as if they were the most precious things in the world. If they got the slightest mark or crease I would take them off and clean them up. I wouldn't run in them or bend my knees if I could help it. I had to be sure that nothing happened to them. On one occasion, when Margaret insisted on me wearing the flares to leave the house, I smuggled the other pair out in a bag. As soon as I was out of sight of the house I dived into the bushes on the golf course and changed them.

There was another family living next door to Alan and Margaret with a daughter called Charlene, who I got on with very well. She went to a girls' school. Her parents, Gary and Diane, had the same respect for Alan that I did and I used to get on with them really well. I wasn't allowed to go out to work any more, but both Margaret and Diane found me jobs to do around their houses and gardens so that I could earn myself some money. I was saving up in the hope that, eventually, I would have enough to buy myself another pair of spare trousers. Money had taken on a new meaning for me. I no longer needed it to get food, because there were always good meals on the table, and I was starting to be given toys so I was like other boys my age there. But I still wanted to earn money for clothes and other things that teenage boys need.

'What are you going to do with all this money you're earning?' Margaret asked me one day.

'I'm going to buy a pair of school trousers,' I said.

She was obviously shocked. 'Why?' she asked.

I took the plunge and told her the truth about the flares. I could see she was puzzled, because Alan wore trousers like that and never had any problems. As I told her how I'd felt in the trousers all through the summer there were tears coming into my eyes and she listened in horrified silence. That weekend we went out together and we bought a twenty-pound pair of trousers, paying half each. She threw away the bell-bottoms for me and suddenly I was free to wear my trousers just like anyone else, no longer living in fear of damaging them because now there was a spare pair I could use until they were cleaned or mended. I felt I was a proper boy at last.

Because I'd put so much effort into my anti-flares campaign, I'd never once had to wear them to the new school and, as a result, I never had any trouble at all. It was like a miracle and once I'd relaxed I started to play sports like water polo, hockey and rugby and made friends, just like everyone else. There were always incidents when someone might try to pick on me or tease me, just as there are in any school. I made sure I never rose to any bait, never responded to any taunts. I remembered to 'count to ten', just as I had been advised all those years before. The last thing I wanted was to be blamed for any sort of trouble, in case I was removed from the school and sent back to my old life. I wasn't one of the really popular guys around the school, but I wasn't one of the nerds either, I was just comfortably in the middle somewhere.

I was now able to relax and settle into my new life. I still loved TV and my favourite time was early Saturday morning before everyone got up when I would go downstairs and sit in front of the TV watching *Raiders of the Lost Ark*. I would sit there completely mesmerized by Indiana Jones in his crusade to save the Ark of the Covenant. To me it was pure adventure, an adventure that completely transported me – my mind was free from everything, just Indiana and I saving the world. I must have seen it over a hundred times at my home.

Margaret and Alan were what is known as an 'emergency' foster family; somewhere where children went until a full-time place could be found for them somewhere else. Their youngest daughter still lived with them. She must have been about twenty, and there were two disabled children who seemed to be there permanently. So it was a full and busy house. Their two eldest children had married and moved to Australia and they'd had one other daughter.

Their son was a bit of a mystery to Alan. Alan Junior

wanted to be an actor and had appeared occasionally in small parts in some of the Australian soap operas. Although he was very proud of him, Alan would rather his boy had followed him into business. When I was with him I felt that we had a real father-and-son relationship, talking about subjects that interested both of us. I got a suspicion that he would have liked to be able to do the same with Alan Junior.

There was a big apple tree in the garden and in the autumn we picked the fruit together, me climbing up amongst the branches and passing the apples back down to him. He taught me never to bang the fruit together otherwise it bruises and rots, so we had to pass it gently from hand to hand. I think it was that motion of me passing him the apples, quite soon after I'd arrived in the house, which formed the bond between us. It made us a team.

I had my own bedroom and although I was much happier during the day, the nightmares still rose up from my subconscious to haunt me once I fell asleep. Margaret would come in response to my screams and would find me curled in a ball, protecting myself against the blows that I expected her to rain down on me, and she would sit on the edge of the bed to calm me. The first time I heard the two of them argue with each other I became frightened and scurried up to my room to hide, but then I realized this was a different sort of arguing to anything I had experienced; that they were never going to hit each other, that they would simply exchange words. Later they would make up with a kiss and cuddle and then life would continue as before. I began to lose some of my fear of confrontation.

I grew to admire Alan more and more as the months went past. He was such a wise man. He seemed so safe because of his height and his grey hair. He'd had a couple of heart attacks before I arrived and so had to take life at a sedate pace. During his working years he'd been up at four every morning, working all hours to build a secure life for his family. Now he kept more leisurely hours, even though he hadn't completely retired.

The garden was T-shaped, and round the corner from the house he had a wooden shed that he sat in, doing the book-keeping for his friends with the help of an old-fashioned adding machine. Sometimes I would just sit in the corner of the office and watch him for hours on end. Whatever question I asked he would always have an answer and it always made sense. I was still apologizing all the time, but I was gradually feeling easier about myself. The concept of business fascinated me. Because I'd worked I understood how hard it was to make money and I wanted to find out how you did it and how you built a business that was good enough to support a family and live a solid life like Alan's. I was brimming with curiosity about everything he did. He taught me new ways to add up and explained how money worked. He was also a keen bridge and poker player and ran a bridge club. During the school holidays I helped set things up for the players and prepare and serve the refreshments through the day. I would always be paid for my efforts, but I would gladly have done it anyway, just to be near him and to be part of the family.

I divided my time between their house and next door. Both Margaret and Diane were wonderful cooks. Margaret actually cooked for the local Women's Institute, and there was always enough to eat at every mealtime. Diane made the best profiteroles I'd ever tasted and once she'd discovered I liked them she made them for me all the time, drenching them in chocolate sauce. So many people were being so kind to me it was hard to believe I'd had to wait so long to find such a normal life. One evening we invited Colin Smith round to supper to thank him for all he'd done. To me it was the icing on the cake.

I was so happy in the house and I dreaded being told it was time to move on to somewhere else and having to start all over again. When they asked if I'd like to stay with them until I finished school I jumped at the chance. I couldn't imagine there could be anywhere better for me to go.

Now and again I would go back to my natural family for visits, just as I had from Yarborough, but I no longer felt I was part of it. I felt like a stranger looking in, and Robert and Julie were no longer there. Then I was told that Gloria and Dennis had split up. I think the violence must have got too much for them both and he just walked out. He was given a housing association flat somewhere and lived alone. Knowing how shy he was I could imagine just how lonely he must be, but I guessed even that was better than being in the house with Gloria all the time. At least he'd be able to drink and listen to Elvis in peace now. I had no sympathy for either of them. As far as I was concerned they deserved whatever misery came their way.

One summer the school arranged a trip for us to the Norfolk Broads for a sailing holiday in small wooden boats. Each boat had four to five boys onboard; one would be a prefect and one would be an experienced sailor. There'd been a list of things we needed for the trip so I even had some new possessions to take with me. I was beside myself with excitement. We set off across the peaceful Broads in a dozen or more little boats, drinking in the fresh air, watching the birds rising up out of the reeds around us and feeling very grown up. It was the most wonderful, liberating experience as we all tried to pretend we were adults now.

While we were out on the water one of the other guys fell overboard fully clothed and disappeared under the boat. There was a moment of horror as we all scanned the water to see where he was and he didn't reappear. Then, after what seemed like an age, he bobbed to the surface at the back of the boat. I knew he wasn't a good swimmer and I'd been doing a lot of swimming by then at school. I didn't even stop to think; I just jumped in and got hold of him, swimming back with him in my arms and pushing him up into the boat. He was bigger than me and heavy with the water in his clothes, as Chris had been when he fell through the ice all those years before, and the others had to help me lift him over the side. No one made a big deal of the affair, but I felt chuffed with myself. I was beginning to feel that I handled myself well when it was necessary, and I thought I'd gained some respect amongst the others, increasing the feeling of camaraderie in the boat. The boy I'd helped had some sweets, which he shared with me. We felt good together, although none of us said anything. It was the trip of a lifetime.

I was still in touch with Gini and Guy and one weekend I went with Guy to his dad's house, which was a beautiful old farmhouse near East Grinstead. It smelled of wood and was full of oak beams and nooks and crannies. His new wife was a great cook and there was tons of food for everyone. It was the sort of house and the sort of lifestyle I'd never experienced before and it took my ambitions forward another gigantic leap as I wandered around, drinking in every detail. I felt that I was entering an adult world. Guy's father was a reporter for the BBC and there was a bunch of journalists at the house for some sort of party that evening; they were all discussing the Falklands War and current affairs in general. As they talked about ships and helicopters and fighting they conjured up a world that was big and exciting, and so far from anything I'd experienced. They were the people who created the world that I'd been watching on the TV screen for so long. They seemed supremely confident and at ease with themselves and the world. Guy's father and his wife had two small children, so there was also a family atmosphere in the house. Outside there were haystacks to play in and a ride-on lawnmower that I was allowed to drive around the croquet lawn. This was the sort of place I would want to bring up any children I might have, somewhere with space and quiet and comfort. Somewhere that feels free and peaceful and smells sweet.

The tiny seeds of ambition inside me, which Alan had been gently nurturing into life, started to blossom that weekend. This was the type of life I wanted to have and I could see now that it was possible, that normal people like Guy and me actually could end up living like this. I just had to work out how to get there from where I was.

15

Going into Business

Throughout my childhood my most pressing problems were how to get through the day without being beaten and how to get enough to eat. Now that I'd finally escaped from Gloria and had grown used to regular square meals, I was keen to get on with my life, to start working towards attaining my dreams, which were coming more into focus as I found out a bit more about how the world worked.

Inspired by Alan's sage advice and by everything I watched or heard about the business world, I decided to go into business for myself at the first opportunity. I was sure it couldn't be that difficult, I just needed a good idea to start me off. At fifteen I set up my own advertising magazine and called it *Eye Catchers*. The idea was to charge local businesses a pound to advertise and I would then print up the ads and deliver them to local houses. A friend called Chey helped me with the deliveries and Alan let us print the magazine up in the back of his office. It felt wonderful to be creating something of my own, something that I believed I could develop into a real business. I had so many plans buzzing around in my head.

We produced three editions before economic realities and a shortage of time got the better of us. We were about twenty quid down on the venture and the pressures of schoolwork during the exam season made it impossible to continue. I was horribly disappointed after the high of seeing the simple little magazine come into existence. But even though it hadn't taken off quite as I'd hoped, it had still whetted my appetite for business. It proved to me that it was possible to start something up from scratch. I could see why it hadn't worked and I was confident I could avoid making the same mistakes next time. I was convinced that if I just worked hard enough I'd be able to succeed in life once I worked out what to do and set my mind to it.

Becoming an entrepreneur wasn't my one and only ambition of course. There were other plans and schemes along the way, sometimes inspired by no more than seeing a good movie. For a short while I flirted with the idea of becoming a pilot, after watching Tom Cruise in *Top Gun*. It looked like the most brilliant way to spend your days and I was sure I would be an ace in no time if I were just given a bit of training. I went to the RAF for an interview but they told me I would have to stay on at school to take O levels and then A levels, and Margaret and Alan weren't prepared to look after me for that long, so I gave that one up.

It was now the middle of the eighties and people kept talking about the fortunes being made in the financial markets in London. The film *Wall Street* was showing in the cinemas and I watched documentaries and news items about the trading pits where everyone was screaming at one another, buying and selling stock. The chaos looked fabulous to me. It looked normal, just like home but without the beatings. It excited me and I knew I could do it well if I was given a chance. If there was one gift Gloria had endowed me with it was a big mouth. I could shout with the best of them. I wanted to become a pit trader. No one needed to have an education to make a fortune here, in fact the papers were always saying it was a profession for 'barrow boys'. There were headlines appearing every day talking about million-pound bonuses and champagne lifestyles for people in their early twenties. I could see no reason why I couldn't become one of them.

Things at school got better and better, feeding my self-confidence about my prospects. When I started there I was in the lower band, with kids who weren't very bright and would take CSEs instead of O levels. Each term I went up a class, having started in the lowest one because of my performance over the previous few years, until just before the examinations when I was only one class below the one taking O levels. I knew that if I'd stayed at Baldwin's Hill and Yarborough I would have been far enough advanced to be doing those exams myself, but I'd lost too much ground in the interim and I didn't have time to catch up. I would be taking CSEs instead.

Despite my improved performance at school, the damage had been done and I still only managed to get CSE grade twos. My teachers, and Margaret and Alan, all wanted me to stay on to try to get grade ones, because they would count the same as O levels and would allow me to get a normal job in a company. But I didn't want a normal job. I didn't want to become a lowly cog in some company, heading off to work on the train each morning, sitting in an office, and coming home exhausted at night, just for a paltry weekly wage. I tried to think what I would be able to do that would make the drudgery worthwhile, and I couldn't think of anything. I wanted to be in control of my own destiny, like Alan had been. I wanted to be a pit trader or an entrepreneur. I thought it would be better to just get out into the world and start working to achieve my dreams rather than worrying about getting some rather average exam results.

I decided to ignore all the good, sensible advice I was being given, and take my chances in the outside world. I'd tasted freedom with the *Eye Catchers* venture. I'd felt the excitement of creating something from nothing, of persuading people to buy advertising space and of actually having control of the product. The experience had lit an entrepreneurial flame inside me, even though it hadn't ended up being successful, and I wanted to try again. I didn't know how or where, but I knew I wanted to get out into the big world that I'd been watching for so many years on television. I was sure that once I was spending all my time looking for opportunities and thinking of ways to make money, I would find them.

We all discussed my plans and it was made clear that if I did leave school I would also have to leave Margaret and Alan's, because they were in the business of fostering children, not adults. In fact as I'd grown older I'd found I'd got closer to Alan but drifted further away from Margaret. I think she preferred dealing with small children and wasn't sure what to do with a teenager who was almost a man. If I did something she disapproved of she used a phrase, 'CHM', which meant 'Council House Mentality'. I heard her use it first when I'd been shouting a bit too loudly in the garden and it stung because there were other people listening, and it reminded me, in a gentler way, of some of the jibes my mother used to throw at me. It made me feel like an outsider again, someone who didn't fit in. As I got older I felt this sort of disapproval from her more often, but I didn't think I deserved it.

She and Alan went on a trip to Australia at one stage to

visit their children, staying away for a couple of months, and during that time I was sent to stay with a friend of Margaret's called Shona. When they got back I noticed a marked change in Margaret's attitude towards me. I think that getting away from it all, and cruising on the *Canberra*, had made her re-evaluate what she wanted to do with the rest of her life and she'd decided that she'd done enough fostering. I felt that she was anxious to get me out of the house and have some quiet time with Alan, who was obviously growing frailer with each year.

I was also told, however, that if I decided to leave school it didn't mean I was going to be put straight out on to the street and expected to fend for myself. I would be helped to get my own place to live. The social services would pay a deposit and two months' rent to get me started, and after that I would support myself. In my naivety, that sounded fine. I imagined I'd be up and working in no time and would be able to pay my rent and support myself easily after two months. I liked the idea of being completely free of everyone and able to live exactly as I wanted. I was so keen to get started I didn't take the time to really think the situation through and ask myself how I was going to get the first job to start me off on my road to riches.

I plunged ahead at full steam. At seventeen I left school and set out to stake my claim in the world, full of high hopes and boundless ambition, confident I would have the whole thing cracked within a few months. From the small ads in the local paper I found a house to share with three other people. It wasn't as nice as Alan and Margaret's, but it wasn't as bad as the two family homes I'd been brought up in. It backed on to the main London to Gatwick rail lines, which made it a bit noisy since trains rattled past pretty much constantly, but I didn't care, I was an early riser anyway. I was given the deposit, the first two months' rent and £200 spending money to support me until I was earning. I was sure I was on my way.

I didn't see that much of the other people in the house. They came and went from whatever jobs they had and we would pass occasionally in the communal rooms, but mostly I kept to my bedroom with the door closed. They were all much older than me and I was putting all my energy into finding a way to make a living. I didn't have time to start a social life.

I was beginning to realize that getting started wasn't going to be quite as easy as I'd first anticipated. I was searching for every vacancy I could find advertised, and ringing or writing to every employer who I thought might be able to use me. But if you have almost no qualifications there aren't that many options on offer; most of the jobs that made the best promises seemed to involve selling things that not many people wanted to buy. I was happy to take anything anyone was willing to offer, but the first job to come my way involved knocking on doors and attempting to sell carpet-cleaning services to housewives who hadn't realized they needed such a service. I didn't intend to do it for long, but I thought it would give me some useful experience and the money would help me to stay afloat until something better came along. It was a harder struggle than I had anticipated, taxing even my gift for the gab.

The salesmen I'd learnt from had worked in the market, where customers had come to them looking for goods to buy, had actually wanted and needed the products they were selling. They had arrived in crowds, with money in their pockets and a willingness to purchase. I was confronting one reluctant customer at a time and having a lot of doors slammed in my face. I'd have to tell the customers it was my birthday and all sorts of rubbish just to get my foot in the door, but still they didn't want to buy the stuff. Who wants to let some smart-talking teenager into their house to sell them something if they can avoid it? No one. Since I was on commission the job wasn't earning me a bean, but it was costing me valuable time and energy and sapping my confidence as I trudged the streets getting rejection after rejection.

I also had a Saturday job at the Homebase DIY Centre in Croydon, which did at least give me a few pounds each week. I'd started there before I left school, having been given a bike on which I cycled down to the Purley Way early every Saturday morning. It was wonderful to have cash that I could spend just as I chose and, as long as I'd been living with Alan and Margaret, it had seemed like a lot of money. Now that it was my only source of income it didn't seem so much.

Still at the back of my mind I had an idealized picture of where I wanted to go with my life. I still envisaged myself escaping to America, where I knew everyone had big dreams, and I still dreamed of finding my fortune in the financial markets, but I could see I had to find a practical way of supporting myself while I pursued these dreams. I was beginning to feel despondent about the amount of time it was taking me to get things moving.

Before I'd left Margaret and Alan's, I'd put some of my earnings towards taking driving lessons, and Margaret had kindly agreed to help me with the rest of the money. I passed my test quite quickly, so that was one skill I did have under my belt. But not many firms want to trust a seventeen-year-old behind the wheel of a company vehicle.

In the first few weeks of being on my own I found the freedom intoxicating. Having money in my pocket and no one to tell me what I should do or where I should go went to my head. The two months that the social services were willing to fund me for seemed like for ever when I first arrived in the house. I couldn't imagine them ever ending. I decided I wanted to try every sort of food I could find: I tested Indian, Chinese, Italian and every other variation – never stopping to work out how much it was costing each week compared to the amount I was earning. If I'd still been in Alan's house he would have pointed out the error of my ways very quickly. But I wasn't, I was on my own, making my own judgements.

Within a few weeks the money was running out and the landlord was mentioning that the rent would soon be due. The two months were nearly up and the pictures in my head of where I wanted to be were beginning to seem a long way from the reality. I'd been working as hard as I knew how, but I seemed to be sliding down a slippery slope towards poverty rather than climbing up towards the wealth and happiness I'd been anticipating.

The two months passed and the rent became due. My pockets were empty and I was suddenly scared. It felt like I had no one to turn to for help. I had to find the money or I'd be homeless, and then I'd never be able to land a job. As long as I had an address I had my foot on the first rung of the ladder. If I slipped off that there would be no safety net to catch me, I would be homeless and unemployable. There was only one option. I went to see Alan to explain what I'd done. I felt so stupid, coming back after only two months with my cap in my hand. He listened to what I had to say, and pointed out the mistakes I'd made, which I already knew. He said he'd lend me a month's rent, but I would have to pay it back. I would have insisted on doing so anyway. I respected him too much to be able to just scrounge from him, and I desperately wanted to win his admiration by succeeding in life. He knew I had to be taught to take responsibility for myself from now on. I was going to have to give up on the carpet-cleaning job because that was obviously not going to work out. I needed to find something sensible to do, so that I had a firm base from which to pursue my ambitions. It was a relief to have been handed another month in which to get started, but the pressure was still on. I now knew how quickly a month could pass.

My only definite income came from the humble Saturday job at Homebase, wandering around the shelves in green dungarees doing whatever I was told and trying to help customers. I decided to increase my hours with them, so that at least I'd have enough to live on. I could have made it a full-time career, but I knew if I wanted to make it to management I was going to have to stay for years, and that still wasn't how I planned to spend my life. However badly things were going, I wasn't ready to give up on my dreams by a long way.

The world was proving to be a bigger, colder and more frightening place than I'd imagined. As my first Christmas on my own approached, I didn't feel I could go back to Alan and Margaret's for the holiday, because I felt they'd done their job with me and it was time to move on, but I didn't have anywhere to move on to. One or two friends invited me to come over on Christmas Day, but I lied and told them I was busy. I didn't want anyone feeling sorry for me. It was the same with birthdays. I'd been used to dealing with all those things on my own as a child, and so I was able to deal with the loneliness now, but it was still hard. Christmas Day is impossible to ignore. It comes at you from every angle with images of families being together round big meals and decorated trees, giving each other presents and enjoying traditions together. If you are sitting alone with a television in a bedsit beside some railway lines, with no money to buy yourself a decent meal, it's impossible not to feel bad.

I'd found I was losing touch with my old school friends anyway because at the times when they were meeting up I had to work. I had to save my money for the rent so I couldn't afford to go to football matches or to the pub whenever they asked, or indulge in any of the other normal social activities that boys of that age go in for. When I got home in the evenings I was usually on my own, just watching the television, eating take-away food and trying to plan a way forward.

When I got to my eighteenth birthday, which I understood was an age when employers would start to consider my applications more seriously, I launched my assault on the money markets. Being a trader was still my dream and I now knew that no one was going to offer me a job unless I made the first approach. I spent hours planning the letter I would write asking for jobs. I did draft after draft, explaining how it was my dream and why I thought I would be good at it and asking for an interview. I hand-wrote over fifty copies of the letter once I was happy with the wording, and sent it to every company in the City that I could find the address of at the library. I made phone calls to get the right names of the people I needed to contact in alien-sounding places like 'personnel departments'.

From the day I sent the letters off I waited in for the postman each morning, hardly able to contain my excitement and anticipation, certain I'd be flooded with offers of interviews. Each day I made new excuses to myself as to why there was nothing, and became optimistic about the next day. In the end, two companies wrote back to say 'no' and the rest ignored me completely. It seemed that in the world I wanted to join, I was virtually invisible.

It was a couple of months before I gave up hoping and accepted that I wasn't going to hear from any more of them, by which time I'd started to formulate a new plan. I was reading everything I could find about the subject, learning about futures trading and options and all the stock exchange terminology, and it was dawning on me that to really make money in the markets you had to use your own capital. That must be the way forward. If I could just find a way of accruing some capital, I could launch myself into the career that I was most interested in without having to rely on anyone else giving me a job. But how to make that seed money, that was the question that seemed to elude me. It was taking every bit of energy I could muster to earn enough to live in one room of a shared house with virtually no outside life at all. Accruing capital seemed like a very distant dream.

It wasn't just that I lacked the necessary education for most careers; I also lacked the aura that confident people have when they go to interviews. I'd learned a lot by watching Alan, but not enough to undo the damage that had been done to my self-esteem in the first fourteen years of my life. The quality that Margaret referred to as my 'council house mentality' must still have been written plainly all over me whenever I wrote letters, made phone calls or turned up for interviews. I had no track record, either educationally or workwise, that I could point to in order to dispel people's first impressions of me. The only jobs that seemed to be open to someone in my position were selling on commission, living by my results.

I started buying the London *Evening Standard* and looking for work in the centre of London. I'd got myself a suit, which must have looked every bit as cheap as it was, and I started going for account management jobs and anything else I could persuade people to interview me for. I was too young for all of them, which gave everyone the perfect excuse for saying no.

'I'll give you this,' one interviewer said as he was turning me down, 'you've got balls.' I took that as a compliment, but it didn't help me move forward.

It wasn't hard to find a certain sort of selling job, but they were soul-crushingly tedious and usually they were only offering payment on results, which seemed unobtainable. I spent some time selling advertising space over the phone for a magazine I'd never heard of, just working from a script and trying to get in as many calls as possible in the hope that a percentage of them were bound to bear fruit. They didn't and it was costing me money just to get to their office. I tried market research, standing in the street asking people questions – more commission that I didn't earn.

My spirits were sinking fast. If this was the only sort of white-collar work I could get, and I couldn't even make a living at that, what on earth was I going to do?

One of the jobs I went for was as a 'sales merchandizer'

for Servis. I think they were offering an £8,000 basic salary and a van, with interviews being held in Birmingham. I sent them a cv in my best writing and rang up to sell myself over the phone. I explained I couldn't afford the ticket up to Birmingham and they agreed to pay my fare. The job involved going round retail outlets checking that all the Servis point-of-sale material was displayed correctly around their washing machines. The interview went like a dream. They invited me back a couple of weeks later and I was offered the job. It was a long way from my dream career, but it was a foot on the next rung of the ladder.

There was a week's training course, where I got to stay in a hotel, which was great because it meant I got proper meals again. I'd been having to cut back a bit in that department in order to pay Alan back his money. One of the things I missed most about moving out of their house was Margaret's cooking. So, every other Friday I went to the Women's Institute market that she used to cook for and bought homemade steak and kidney pies and biscuits. Even though Margaret had stopped cooking for them herself, I still knew many of the other old ladies down there and they'd always look after me.

That hotel room in Birmingham seemed like the height of luxury to me. Although I'd been on holiday a couple of times with Margaret and some other kids, I'd never stayed in a hotel on my own or had a room like this to myself. At the end of the course I got to drive my Servis van back home so that I'd have it there to do my rounds to the retailers. It was the first time I'd driven since passing my test about a year before and I was having terrible trouble remembering all the stuff I'd been taught. I could see the fleet manager watching me with a worried expression as the van crawled out of the service area. I'd forgotten to change the mirrors and couldn't see anything except sky in any direction, but I wasn't going to stop and readjust them in front of everyone.

I drove out in search of the motorway with my suit on and my briefcase and equipment in the back and I felt like I'd finally arrived. When I eventually found the motorway I thought I'd take it easy in the slow lane, but that only lasted about five minutes before I was into the fast lane with my foot on the floor. I had a job and a vehicle and I was ready to go places now.

I stayed with Servis for about six months and I learnt a lot. The most important lesson, however, was that if I wanted to make anything of myself in life it was going to have to be through selling. That was going to be the way in which I'd get together the capital I needed to pursue my real dreams. I realized that everyone had to sell something in order to survive, and that I just had to learn to do it better than anyone else.

When I was passed over by Servis for a promotion to selling that I thought I deserved, I decided it was time to move on and I went to Konica, to train for selling photocopiers. I soon realized I wasn't going to make enough money there and moved on again to another company that people in the business were all talking about. I didn't enjoy the job as much as the Servis job, but it did teach me that in order to make decent money you have to sell direct to companies and not be a 'rep'. There were senior salesmen working at this place who earned over £100,000 a year. There were even some ex-money markets people there, earning more than they had from their trading. It seemed I had finally got myself to the right place at the right time.

When I started there I worked unbelievably hard, trudging the streets looking for business. My efforts paid off because I made £5,000 in my first month, which I then spent in clubs and pubs. I felt certain I was on a roll now. If I could make that much in just a month, I would have no trouble doing it again. I'd broken through the barriers that had been holding me back and nothing would stop me now. My bank obviously agreed and immediately granted me an overdraft facility and I was offered credit everywhere I turned. Before long I was driving a three-litre Supra car and living like a king, all on credit. It was 1989 and boom time in the UK.

The results of the first month, however, proved to be something of a freak. I was still doing better than I'd ever done in my life, but I was not earning as fast as I was spending and the debts were mounting up. All the good advice I'd taken from Alan over the years was forgotten in a surge of overconfidence and relief at finally having broken out of the cycle of poor education and bad beginnings. I'd lost focus on my dreams.

A year later the photocopying industry crashed. There was a problem with the paying of commission within the company. I lost my job, but the debts were still there. I tumbled off the ladder again, back to where I'd started, but with even fewer illusions.

16

Slipping Beyond the Law

My life by that time had changed a great deal, but it was all built on sand. By the time my job in the photocopying business had vanished I'd moved house and was sharing with a guy I'd met at the company. I was also spending time at another friend's house in Horley, a town near Gatwick, and there I'd met up with a man called Paul, who worked for one of the big car rental companies and lived on the same estate.

One day Paul came round to the house driving a brand-new Mercedes S-Class; a seriously luxurious car. It belonged to the rental company he worked for but he'd found a way of getting it for his own personal use without anyone knowing. The way the scam worked was that the car had been booked into the repair shop, although there was nothing wrong with it. Because no one had checked up on it after that, Paul had then been able to drive it away from the repair shop without anyone in the company noticing it had gone. I was deeply impressed by this sleight of hand and by how easy it appeared to have been.

'I've got another car at home,' Paul said. 'Do you want this one to use?'

He explained it was better for him to have the Mercedes driven around than for it to be parked all the time near his house. He didn't want to be driving around in such a luxurious car in case he was spotted by someone from his work. The other car was much less conspicuous.

Since I was by then without any sort of vehicle I accepted the offer gratefully. The car was a revelation, a hundred times better than anything I'd ever driven before. Gliding around the area in such luxury lifted my dampened spirits and reminded me just how much I wanted to be successful, so that I could own these sorts of nice things for myself. Being inside a powerful, solidly built car makes you feel invulnerable and capable of anything. I liked that feeling and wanted more of it.

Since working in London I'd started doing some sparring at a boxing club in the area to keep myself fit and to let out some of the anger that was still trapped inside me. Letting off steam with the punch bag always made me feel a lot better and now took my mind off the fact that I had large debts, no money or income with which to deal with them in the foreseeable future and couldn't find a job. It was almost like being back where I had been at the beginning, since working as a salesman for a photocopying company didn't qualify me for any other sort of job apart from the commission-only selling jobs I'd tried in the past and found to be useless.

I was meeting a lot of different people around the club and one of them spotted the car as I was climbing into it to go home. We started talking and the conversation quickly got on to the Merc. I explained it wasn't mine, that I was just using it from the rental company before it went in for repair.

'I know someone who would take a car like that off your hands,' he said. 'If you ever needed some quick money.'

'Yeah?' I replied casually. 'How much do you think he'd be willing to pay?'

'Couple of grand, I should think.'

By that time I was desperately in need of money to pay off the debts that I'd stupidly allowed to build up, so I promised to give the suggestion some thought. I went back to Paul in Horley and told him what this guy had said.

'They say we can get a couple of grand for this car,' I said.

'Well, no one at the company knows it's gone,' Paul said. 'So we might as well.'

The decision was taken and arrangements were made by telephone. We were told to take the car a few days later and park near a roundabout in Chertsey. The man we were dealing with was coming down from South London and would meet us there. We drove to the designated place in both cars. I took mine to the location they'd described to us and Paul parked his round the corner and came to sit with me. Both of us were quiet and jumpy as we looked around, trying to predict what was likely to happen next. Not only were we scared of getting caught by the police, we were also nervous about who we were due to be meeting. We knew they were not going to be people who you messed with. What if they just took the car and didn't give us our money? What if they didn't turn up? What if the police turned up and wanted to know what we were up to? I was very tempted to forget the whole thing and just drive away, but then I remembered how much I needed the money. And anyway, I'd given these people my word I would be there.

There were dozens of unanswerable questions going round and round in my head as I watched the roads outside and I wished I had never got involved. But it was too late to back out now. We were committed to going through with it, and the money was going to solve a lot of immediate problems.

We sat for a while in this state of tension, watching the traffic going by, trying to work out which car would be the one coming to see us. An anonymous looking saloon containing four men went past.

'That looked like them,' I said.

'Nah,' Paul shook his head. 'They've driven on.'

'They're back,' I said as the car reappeared on the round-about and cruised past once more, the men inside not giving us a second look.

'What are they playing at?' Paul wondered.

'Just checking us out, I guess. Making sure no one else is watching.'

The car circled the roundabout slowly a few more times and we could see that now they were looking at us. We still had no way of knowing what was going to happen next. The game went on for about ten minutes as they checked the coast was clear and no one else was lying in wait. Then the car pulled up a few yards away from us. Two of the men got out and walked briskly over. The remaining men drove away immediately.

We climbed out of the car to meet them. A white envelope was pushed into my hand and the keys were taken away. No eye contact was made. The Mercedes had gone within seconds and we were left standing on our own, wondering what had happened. We made our way quickly to where we'd left Paul's car and drove home. I opened the envelope as we drove and checked the money was there. It was. I felt a mixture of relief that it was over and that we had the money, and disquiet that I'd slipped over the law in order to make a living. I told Paul I was nervous the car was going to be traced back to us.

'How can they?' he wanted to know. 'No one even knows it's gone from the company. When they do find out, how would they trace it to us?'

'The problem is, I haven't got anything to drive around in now,' I pointed out.

'I'll sort you out something,' he promised.

True to his word, he got me another car, a more modest Ford this time, for my own use, and a few days later I lost the key, which also had the car's alarm on it. I rang Paul up and told him my problem.

'Well, I can't get a new key cut at work,' he said, 'or they'll notice the car's out and start asking questions. I'll get you the key number and you can get it cut somewhere else.'

An hour later he rang back with the key number. I went down to a local key-cutting service, gave them the number Paul had dictated to me and told them it was for a Ford. They didn't ask any more questions, they just did as I asked and gave me the key. I couldn't believe it was that simple, although the full implications of it didn't strike me immediately.

A few weeks after we'd disposed of the Mercedes the garage owner who'd taken it phoned up out of the blue. I was a little unnerved to hear from him at first, wondering if there was a problem, not really comfortable with the idea that someone like him knew how to find me so easily. But his tone was friendly and he didn't seem worried about anything. We chatted about nothing much for a few minutes and then he got to the point.

'If you can get hold of a car like that one,' he said, very reasonably, 'you should be able to get hold of others to order.' We decided to meet a few days later in a pub. He had given me a great deal of food for thought. By then the thousand pounds I had got from the Mercedes had gone but none of my debt problems had. I still hadn't been able to find any other way to earn a living. At the same time I was uncomfortable about being involved with people who obviously operated a long way outside the law.

'I can't steal cars,' I told him when we met. 'I just wouldn't be able to do it.'

In my mind there was all the difference in the world between selling something that had come into my possession by dubious means and actually going out stealing things that belonged to other people. The fact that no one at the company had even missed the Mercedes made me feel better about profiting from its disappearance. The act seemed to be one step removed from actually stealing from another person.

'You don't have to go round breaking into them in the street,' he laughed, cajoling me along, making me feel foolish for holding such scruples. 'You could work with your friend, getting them out of his company.'

As he was talking an idea was going through my head. If Paul could get me the key numbers to other cars, and he could also book them in for repairs, I could just walk in and get them from wherever he had them parked up. I told my contact I'd think about it and get back to him.

That evening Paul and I went out for a drink and I told him about the call and about my idea. He thought about it for a few minutes and agreed he could see that the system might work. The garage owner in South London needed to order cars of certain makes and colours to fit the profiles of wrecks that had been brought in and registration papers that he had in his possession. If we could find cars to match his specifications we could supply him.

'Let's try it,' Paul said when we'd talked round every angle of the idea and not found any snags.

'Okay, I'll ring him back,' I agreed, 'and tell him we'll give it a go. I won't make any promises, just say we'll try it out.'

A few days later the garage owner rang with a make and colour he needed. I rang Paul and passed the information on. He then rang back with a key number of a vehicle that fitted the description and a location where I would be able to find it. I got the key cut and went to collect the car, delivering it to a street close to the garage, leaving the key underneath for them to pick up once they'd received a call. The system worked like a charm. They paid us on time and ordered another car a couple of weeks later. We'd created a business for ourselves, supplying cars to order.

Word spreads about this sort of thing in certain circles and I began to get a reputation as someone who could get things that people wanted. I didn't disillusion anyone, just allowed the rumours to persist. The car deals were putting enough money in my pocket to live on, but not much more. I should have been more worried about them than I was, but I rationalized it away as the only person getting hurt was an anonymous car rental company, who would be claiming off insurance anyway. It seemed like a relatively harmless crime, at least that was how I justified it to myself.

Having discovered I had a skill and a growing reputation I began to think of ways of expanding it into other areas that might pay. I was spending a fair bit of time in pubs and clubs, where you can't help but meet a variety of different people. Anyone I met who was involved in the management side, I tried to find out what they wanted, to see if there were other things I might be able to supply in exchange for cash. Acquiring the cars was taking almost no time at all and I was keen to work hard if anyone wanted to use my services.

One thing led to another and I found there was an endless appetite in the club trade for cheap alcohol and cigarettes. I got to know the most influential local club and bar owners and found out what they needed. On the whole they seemed to be willing to take anything as long as it was the right price. I'd then go out and source the products from other contacts who were bringing them in from different places and needed to get rid of them quickly. I'd become a middle-man, doing the deals that the people running the clubs didn't have time to do for themselves and didn't want to get involved with. I would take a cut on each deal.

A lot of my business transactions took place in the car parks of those anonymous service stations dotted along the motorways, where lorries, vans and cars intermingle and no one knows anyone else. In these transient places it was easy to exchange vehicles or move a few crates around without attracting any attention, especially after dark. I'd stumbled into a parallel business world; living alongside the legitimate business travellers, but invisible to anyone who isn't part of it, moving goods between those who have them and those who want them with no paperwork, being paid in nothing but cash.

My operations didn't always go smoothly. There was one incident where I somehow ended up with the wrong van and had a load of seafood to dispose of instead of drink. The neighbours all dined on lobster for several weeks.

It doesn't take long before you get a reputation in this

line of work. The criminal world is small and word travels through it quickly. If you're known to have money to spend and contacts to sell to, people will get in touch, offering to supply things. I was aware that the club owners were people you couldn't mess around with, hard businessmen who did whatever was necessary to stay in business and turn a profit. I made sure I never made promises I couldn't fulfil and I always owned up quickly if I wasn't able to get something they wanted. It was business to me, plain and simple, getting cash to live on and to help pay off my debts. I behaved as professionally as if I was in a legitimate business and people respected me for it. I became known as 'The Kid'. I would turn up at a club and calls would be put through to the owners from the doors: 'The Kid's here'. I'd be ushered quickly through. I was useful to them and I didn't mess them about and they responded to that.

Because I provided the club owners with a good service I found that I'd become 'connected'. Word got about and it was generally known that 'The Kid' was protected by powerful people, and so my reputation grew. Very few people interfered with me because they knew who my contacts were. I got into a couple of fights in bars and I won very quickly, partly because I'd been training at the boxing club and was very fit, but also because I'd learnt from my parents to hit hard and fast. As a result I also gained a reputation for being hard myself, which was only partly deserved.

I would never have had the temperament to be a professional boxer because as soon as someone hit me or upset me I'd immediately hit back with no forethought or subtlety, using every ounce of strength I could muster. The anger that had built up in the first twenty years of my life was just sitting there waiting for someone to disturb it. I didn't play any games or exercise any strategic thinking when I fought, which meant any drunk picking a fight with me in a bar because they thought I was a bit young and flash got hit much quicker and harder than they'd expected. But these were isolated incidents. You only have to knock someone out once or twice for word to get around and people to steer clear. Almost nobody gave me any trouble at all. Because I'd been so damaged as a child, and knew I could survive, I wasn't frightened of anything. I wasn't even frightened of dying. When you've got nothing to lose you're in a pretty strong position in many ways. Perhaps other people could sense that about me, perhaps that was why they showed me the respect they did.

More people came to me asking for things as the months went by, and the more deals I was able to put together, all of them putting cash in my pocket. I was staying afloat, I was living the good life, out every night and driving a flash motor, but it was still a business built on sand. I still had no capital or substance behind me. It was all wads of cash passing from hand to hand, creating an illusion of big money and affluence, when in fact it was just quick turnover, small profits and a lot of flash spending. I wasn't building up the money that I needed for all the dreams that now seemed to be on hold.

Despite the lack of solid money, I felt much more secure and protected than I ever had in the legitimate business world I'd tried to make a living in first. Now there were powerful people who had a vested interest in looking after me; that made me feel confident and comfortable. As long as I could get them what they wanted they didn't want any harm to befall me. I loved the feeling of being able to walk past queues waiting to get into clubs and being let straight in. I imagined that everyone left outside was wondering who I was. After a lifetime of being the boy on the outside watching everyone else having a life, I was finally accepted and on the inside. That was a good feeling. I belonged somewhere at last, even if I was only just keeping myself above water financially.

I still kept myself to myself, even when I was socializing. I never told anyone exactly what I was up to, because I reckoned if no one knew then no one could blab on me. I didn't expect to stay in this world for ever, I would be wanting to go back to the straight world as soon as I could get something legitimate together, and so I didn't want to be saddled with any sort of criminal record. I knew that the criminal life wasn't for me, because it was only a matter of time before I would be caught doing something, but I couldn't yet see a way out into the legitimate world.

The car business stopped when Paul left the rental company, and I concentrated on supplying drink to club owners. Although I enjoyed the feeling of being able to strut around the clubs, protected and respected, I was desperate to find a way into a proper business, but I knew it was still a matter of raising a lump of capital with which to back myself. I was only twenty-one by then, but I felt like I'd been fighting to get a foothold in the business world for ever.

17

Bereavement and Disappointment

While I was working as a deal turner I got back in contact with Margaret and Alan. I'd matured a lot since leaving them, having learned to stand on my own two feet, even if it wasn't yet in the way I'd hoped. It put our relationship on a different footing, strengthened it even. Despite my rocky start I'd managed to survive in the outside world and that made me feel like I'd achieved something and could go back with my head held high. They didn't have to know what I was doing; they just saw the surface, the young man who seemed to be looking after himself in the world. They didn't ask me any questions about my work; maybe Alan could guess the sort of things I did.

He'd suffered another heart attack, which upset me badly, and it was beginning to look as if he wasn't going to survive much longer. He wasn't getting out much and it was obvious that he was tired most of the time. There were plans being laid for him and Margaret to spend more time in Australia with the children and grandchildren who lived out there. They'd been trying to sell their house, but without much luck since the property market was depressed. I made sure I spent as much time as possible with Alan because I was afraid I wouldn't have him around for much longer. I went round to the house at every opportunity. Sometimes we'd just sit together in the garden without saying much, comfortable in the knowledge that the other one was there. I went back to staying with them some nights and going off to work from there. One morning, as I left the house, I glanced up and saw him watching me from his bedroom window.

'You take care of yourself,' he called down, as if he knew something was going to happen. I waved back and went to work with a strange feeling of disquiet in the pit of my stomach, unsure why I felt so bad.

When I got home that afternoon I could tell there was a sombre mood in the house the moment I came in through the front door. I could hear people talking in subdued voices. Margaret was in the kitchen with Gary from next door and her youngest daughter, Donna. The disquiet I'd been feeling all day stirred into a painful foreboding. I knew I was about to find out something that would hurt a lot. I pushed open the door and they turned to look at me with faces that explained everything. As I listened in stunned silence they told me that Alan had died playing bridge, the thing he enjoyed more than anything else. Even though I'd been expecting it, the news hit me like a punch in the face. I couldn't think of anything to say, just turned on my heel and walked out of the room, wanting to get away from everyone else so that I could let my feelings out without inhibition. I walked through to the lounge and sat in his favourite chair, put a cushion to my face and wept uncontrollably. Gary came through a little later and patted me on the shoulder, trying to console me, but I was inconsolable. I had no idea how I was going to cope with the grief that was churning around inside me. More than anyone else, Alan had given me the time and support and love that had been missing from my life for so long. I'd wanted so much to have him around to watch as I moved up in the world and achieved all the things I wanted to achieve, but now he'd gone and there would be no more chats in his workroom or bridge parties or quiet afternoons in the garden. He would never see me amount to anything at all, never know how big a part he had played in my life. There were so many things I wished I had said to him, and now it was too late.

I found the funeral particularly difficult because, whereas I'd felt like we had a father-and-son relationship when we were together, I was now relegated to being a friend of the family, no longer part of the immediate family. I did understand this from their point of view. But although I wasn't Alan's real son he'd been more of a real father to me than Dennis. I wouldn't have expected anything else, but being pushed to the sidelines left me with an empty feeling in my stomach, reminded me that I didn't really belong anywhere.

All through the service I couldn't stop crying. It was as if the floodgates had finally been lifted after all the years of holding back the tears and there was no way of closing them again. I found the idea of his body being burnt unbearable. When the coffin rolled away through the doors to the furnace I was completely unable to control myself. I couldn't understand how anyone could be burning the body of someone they loved. I remembered the feeling of being safe in the arms of the fireman as a tiny child and this seemed to go against all that I'd felt that night. Gary tried to comfort me again outside the crematorium but there was little he could do. I covered my eyes with sunglasses and stayed silent.

When we got back to the house again I went upstairs and lay on my bed. I couldn't face mixing with the others downstairs, making polite conversation and handing round sandwiches. I didn't want people to see how much I'd been crying.

Margaret was very businesslike about everything. I think they must both have known it was coming because they'd already transferred all their joint assets over to her. Once the funeral was over she just wanted to pack up and move down to Australia to be where most of her family was, and to put her past behind her. I suggested that if she wanted to get rid of the house quickly, I'd buy it from her to take it off her hands. I don't know how I thought I was going to do it. I guess it was just one of those things you say without expecting anything to come of it. I certainly didn't have the money to run it, let alone buy it, but perhaps I thought I'd work that one out when the time came. Margaret knew enough about my situation to be aware I didn't have the sort of money for buying houses, and she suggested that if I did buy the house from her, she'd loan me £30,000 to start a business.

'It's what Alan would have wanted,' she told me, and I felt choked with emotion.

The moment she suggested it I could see this was my way forward, and that it would have been what Alan would have wanted, with Margaret and I both helping each other to put our lives in order. The £30,000 was exactly the sort of capital I felt I needed to get myself launched into a legitimate business. I could imagine Alan would have approved, given his grasp of business and of the need to have money behind you. If I had that sort of capital to work with I could stop dashing around making a few quid here and a few quid there, and concentrate on making the money work for me, and I'd have something to make the mortgage repayments on the house while I got established. I could give up living on the edge of the law, and really start to build something. It would be the stepping-stone I needed to get to the next stage of my life and I accepted the offer gratefully. I knew that I could work hard and that with the money I would be able to create something that I could grow and build. I was so looking forward to the chance to prove what I was capable of. I already had my eyes on a business. A friend of mine had introduced me to a gentleman who wanted to sell his bar. It was the kind of business that I felt would put me on the road to the success that I wanted in a legitimate line of work. I also liked the sort of life which owning a bar would provide. It would give me a fixed place in the world.

It was not going to be a straightforward deal between Margaret and me by any means. The house was on the market at £125,000 and until Margaret was in a position to give me the loan, I didn't even have the money to pay for stamp duty. But she wouldn't have any money to give me until I'd managed to get a mortgage in order to pay her for the house. With no money for a deposit and no steady income, getting a mortgage was going to be difficult. It was a chicken and egg situation. A friend of mine knew about mortgages and said I could get a 90 per cent one if I could just prove my income, and if Margaret told them the house was actually going for £145,000 and that I had already paid her a £20,000 deposit. I don't know how I proved I had an income, but I did. It was a fraud. But I had no choice if I wanted to lift myself back to the legitimate side of life.

All through the negotiations I kept checking with Margaret that the loan was still on, to the point where I think I was starting to annoy her.

Interest rates were high and the mortgage was going to be costing me over £1,000 a month, but I was convinced I could make the £30,000 work for me and earn me enough to cover it. Margaret went off to Australia just before we completed the deal. The day before we exchanged contracts I spoke to her on the phone in Sydney and I asked again, 'Am I still all right for this £30,000? I can't afford this house without it.'

She assured me it would all be sorted out.

Two days later, with the deal on the house completed, I rang her again to ask about the loan. She told me she'd spoken to her lawyer and been advised against giving me the money. I felt the world caving in around my head as her words sank in. Not only could I see my dreams of starting the business and being truly independent disappearing in smoke, I could also see that I now had outgoings of over £1,000 a month and not enough income to cover them.

I phoned back again a bit later to plead with her and to try to find out why she was doing such a cruel thing.

'I haven't even got the money for the stamp duty or the first mortgage payment,' I said.

She put the phone down on the side, without hanging up, and walked away. I was stuck with an open line to Australia and no one to speak to.

I moved into the house, because at least then I wasn't paying out any rent, but it was a sad experience. All the furniture had gone, missing pictures leaving bare patches on the walls, naked light bulbs hanging from the ceilings and a few old curtains and carpets, now robbed of their previously homely feel, just looking tired and shabby. The only pieces of furniture left were my bed and a chair.

It was coming up to Christmas and I had to spend the

festive season alone in the empty house with no money and my dreams a distant glimmer. I had never felt so lonely in my life. My deal for the bar was put on hold and I couldn't see how I could get it up and going again. My disappointment was overwhelming.

18

Down to Bare Knuckles

I was still boxing to keep fit and took out my frustrations on the punch bag. I would never have been able to become a professional because of my temperament, but I was still able to handle myself. I needed a way to vent my frustrations since everything else in my life was going from bad to worse. There were some problems with the law in the area where I lived and worked and the club owners I'd been supplying all went to ground, causing my drinks business to dry up overnight. There were no hard feelings; they just didn't want to buy anything that might be remotely dodgy. I suddenly had no income at all, not even cash in my pocket to buy food, and the debts were building up every day at the house.

Some people knew that I was desperate to earn some money and I had been approached a few weeks before by a guy called Johnny. I'd seen him around a few times but didn't know much about him.

'You're a good fighter,' he said matter-of-factly. 'If you ever need money, I might be able to offer you some work.'

He gave me his number and I put it into my pocket without ever thinking I'd do anything about it. I knew what he was talking about; illegal fights, or 'bare-knuckle' as they're known, where there were no rules except destroying your opponent as quickly and brutally as possible. At that stage I was still concentrating on trying to keep the drinks business going. Now, however, a few weeks later, with mortgage payments and household bills piling up around me, I needed to scrape together money in any way I could if I didn't want to lose everything and be in debt for years to come. I called the number he'd given me, reminded him who I was and told him I needed money.

'Well,' he said, 'if you can handle yourself, maybe you could have a fight or something.'

I didn't think that much of it. I felt I'd tried everything else, why not try this?

'Okay,' I said. 'How much do I get paid?'

'A hundred and fifty if you win, nothing if you lose.'

'Okay. What do I wear?' Looking back, it was a strange thing to ask, but it was the only thing that came into my head.

'Just tracksuit bottoms and T-shirt,' he said.

Once he'd hung up I began to imagine what it might be like. It might be fun to fight; to be up in a ring in some crowded, smoky, illegal den with onlookers screaming and shouting, urging me on, people laying bets and laughing and having a good time. The idea began to grow on me, taking on a sort of seedy romanticism and glamour.

It was arranged that I'd be picked up a few evenings later around King's Cross somewhere. It was getting dark as I waited on a street corner until the car pulled up and I got in. I was already feeling apprehensive; not knowing where I was going or what was going to happen. There were several men in the car and we drove out of London on one of the main routes for about an hour. No one spoke much. The last of the daylight faded and we reached the ___ the streetlights. The night was getting ___

We turned off the main roads and drove through a built-up area on to a narrow, unmade track. We went over a hill and started to descend to an area that wasn't overlooked by any houses. I now had no idea where I was. I began to feel nervous, the butterflies churning in my stomach. Eventually we came out on to a field. This was beginning to look very different to the scene I'd been imagining.

There were eight cars pulled up facing into a circle as we bumped across the grass to join them. The men who'd come in the cars were standing around, smoking and talking in quiet voices. I guess they were making bets, but I was more interested in trying to work out what was going to happen to me. The cars' headlights illuminated the 'ring' in which the fight would take place. My opponent was already stripped down to the waist and waiting. He was a bit taller and older than me and didn't seem to have that much muscle on him, but he was covered in tattoos. I knew he'd be happy to hurt me in any way he could and I just had to make sure I got him first.

'What happens?' I asked Johnny, my contact.

'Just get on with it,' he grunted.

There was no whistle or bell or anything to signify the fight had started. I pulled off my jacket and walked towards my opponent. As I got close I noticed he smelt. It was as if he'd been working with horseshit all day and had come straight from there without washing. We grabbed each other, landing punches and kicks wherever we could. I was immediately angry and unable to hold back any of my punches. I just wanted to hurt him badly. I managed to get a grip on his legs and jerk them out from under him. The moment he was down on the floor I stamped on his head. I kept kicking and punching as fast and as hard as I could, determined not to let him get up again. If he couldn't get up I'd won. The audience made no sound as they watched. They didn't cheer or boo or shout anything at all; or, if they did, I didn't hear them. They just watched us getting on with the job.

It was all over in a couple of minutes. My T-shirt was ripped and my tracksuit bottoms were covered in mud. I felt shattered. The men got back into their cars and drove away. Johnny gave me my money and I sank silently into the car they'd brought me in. The ride back was as quiet as the ride down had been. They dropped me back at King's Cross and I made my way wearily home. I had a few cuts on my face but nothing to alarm anyone who might see me. It had been nothing like I'd imagined and I felt bad about what I'd done to the other guy, but I knew he'd have done the same to me if he'd been able to. It had been a reasonably easy night's work.

Johnny rang again a couple of weeks later to see if I wanted another fight. I still needed the money and the memory of the first one was already fading, so I said yes. The pick-up routine was the same and once we were at the location we waited in the car for a few minutes, surveying the scene. My opponent was sitting in another car a little way away. We stared at each other through the car windows, trying to weigh one another up. This time there were more cars forming the ring, and there were some women amongst the onlookers. They seemed like gypsies to me, but I didn't take much notice of them, concentrating on what I was going to be doing. It was as if the first fight had just been a trial and now I was being given a bigger audience. Everyone seemed to be waiting for someone else to make the first move. I wanted to get it over with so I opened the car door and got out. It was as if I'd given a signal and all the other car doors opened as people got out to watch.

I knew what to do this time. I walked straight over to my opponent. He was quite good looking, with dark hair and a toned body. Unlike the first guy, this one looked fit. I smacked him in the face with all my strength. I would guess he was in his late twenties, a little bit taller than me again. I was pretty fit myself from my training and he went down from the first punch. I think I may have broken his nose. There was certainly a lot of blood coming out of it. His tooth had split my knuckle right through to the bone; I heard the skin ripping open as I punched but I didn't feel a thing. I kept hitting him and every time I made contact a spurt of blood came out of my knuckle. He never recovered from the first blow and within what seemed like no time I'd taken him out and he was lying motionless on the ground. When I was sure he wasn't getting up again I looked at my hand and saw the white of the knucklebone poking through the flesh. The pain began to get through to me.

I'd won my money again and this time they gave me a lift back to Coulsdon, dropping me on the A23, just off the motorway, and leaving me to walk back to the house. Once I was inside I sat down and cried at the way my life was going. All the emotions I'd been holding in came flooding out. I'd had so many dreams and tried everything I could think of to make a success of my life, but now I was living in a deserted house, deep in debt and having to fight for pocket money. The thought occurred to me that I just might not be able to do anything better, that I'd been kidding myself all along to think I could ever amount to anything. There was no one I could turn to for help or advice because

Alan was dead and I certainly couldn't go back to my parents. I was no longer close to any of my school friends, and the business people who were my new acquaintances were not the sort of people to go pleading to. I felt completely alone. By the time I got to bed the pain from my hand was excruciating and there was no chance I'd be able to sleep.

In the morning I took myself down to the local hospital and they stitched the wound up for me. They didn't ask any awkward questions.

19

From Bad to Worse

One of my favourite haunts for food when I was living back at Alan's old house was the local fish and chip shop. I'd noticed there were three guys who always seemed to be standing outside the shop. I could tell they were as thick as porridge but I had no reason to speak to them about anything so I didn't give them a second thought. There was also a black guy living locally, who was slightly disabled. I didn't know him either, had never spoken to him, but I noticed the three idiots messing around behind him one time, taking the mickey out of the way he walked. None of it was any of my business, since I didn't know any of them, but the sight of it grated somewhere deep inside my head. Maybe it reminded me of when I was a child being taunted by the other children, or of seeing Kimberley trapped in the corner of the room by the boys at Yarborough. I didn't do anything about it, but the incident played on my mind, making me feel slightly sickened when I thought about it. Another time I was driving past at the same time of day and I saw exactly the same thing happening. They were taking the mickey out of him behind his back, which seemed well out of order. I parked the car and went into the shop.

'Give me a bag of chips, will you?' I said to the boy behind the counter. 'And make them hot ones.'

'These are hot,' he said.

'No,' I said, 'I want them still with boiling oil on them. I'll pay you extra.'

He didn't ask any more questions, just did what I asked. I covered the boiling hot chips in salt and vinegar, walked outside and smashed them straight into the face of the biggest of the three, who seemed to be the leader, and then I went after the other two.

'You ever pick on him again,' I warned, 'and I'll fucking kill you.'

I knew I shouldn't be getting involved, but I also knew no one else would if I didn't, and the disabled guy deserved to be able to walk home each day without having to put up with abuse from a bunch of clowns. I sometimes saw them round the area after that, but I never saw them outside the chip shop again.

About a month after my second bare-knuckle fight, when my hand was beginning to heal, Johnny was on the phone again. This time he had a better offer for me. In this fight I'd get a hundred and fifty pounds if I lost and a thousand if I won. I presumed this meant there was something even dodgier than usual about the deal. If they were willing to pay me even if I lost, this fight was probably going to go to a level of viciousness I hadn't had to deal with before. But if I won a grand, that would help me with the mortgage payment that month and buy me some more time in the house to think of some way to get myself out of trouble. By this time the mortgage company was becoming suspicious of why I hadn't paid anything, not even the first instalment, and lawyers were demanding payment for the stamp duty on the house. I agreed to take on the fight.

I was picked up in King's Cross again and driven out to the same place. This time there must have been thirty cars in the circle. Something much bigger was going on and I felt uneasy. I'd strapped my knuckle together with some sticky tape. I knew it was bound to hurt, so I'd swallowed several painkillers in the car in preparation. The moment I saw my opponent I knew I'd been set up. He was completely different to the first two. The others must have been used to build my confidence and make me feel I could win against anyone they found for me. No one who'd seen this guy in advance would have volunteered to fight him. He looked more like an animal than a man. He had no neck and hardly any teeth. His skin was as thick and hard as cheap leather work boots. He was shorter than me but built like a bear.

I glanced around at the onlookers. There were a lot of serious faces. There must have been real money being betted on this one. It was obvious this guy was a professional. I knew they wouldn't let me back out now. If I tried to call off the fight the crowd would beat me up as well as my opponent. There was no option but to try to bring him down quickly or prepare myself for a beating.

I went in as hard and fast as I had the time before, smacking him with all my strength, but it made no impact whatsoever; I might as well have punched a brick wall. I could tell there was nothing I could do to hurt this man. He grabbed me like I was a child and punched me so hard my head seemed to explode. Before the explosion had even finished he headbutted me and a giant silver flash went off in my face. I went down like a sack of rags and he didn't let up for a second, punching, kicking, dragging me around in the dirt. He was enjoying himself. Everywhere I turned he was there, with the glare of car headlights behind him, blinding me as I reeled about in search of an escape route.

At one stage I managed to pull myself to my feet, thinking

I might be able to make a run for it, but my legs wouldn't work. He came at me again and I felt myself being lifted off the ground and bent backwards over the bonnet of one of the cars. A metal emblem jabbed into the base of my spine like a blunt knife. I'd thought Gloria was bad, but this beating was beyond anything I'd ever experienced. As I slid to the ground again I responded just as I had as a child, curling myself into a ball to protect my vital organs and waiting for it all to be over. After a while the blows didn't actually create pain as they fell, it was more like the distant thuds of bombs dropping. I could feel their impact on me, breaking my skin and my bones, but I was spared the pain. That would come later, when the numbness had worn off.

Then I must have passed out because I don't remember anything until I came round to find every inch of my head and body throbbing. I was desperately thirsty but when I tried to speak my lips were too swollen to move. My eyes were virtually closed up as I tried to peer around and see what was happening and where I might be able to find comfort. Some of the cars were already leaving with roars of exhaust fumes and sprays of dirt. There was no sign of Johnny. I later discovered he'd betted on me on the first two fights, deliberately building my reputation by putting me against people I could easily beat, and then he'd betted against me on the third fight, knowing that I hadn't a hope. He must also have known there was no chance I would ever want to fight again, and so there was no reason to help me get home. Someone I'd never seen before gave me my £150 loser's fee.

My opponent was still there and now he'd won his money and spent his aggression he was as nice as pie to me. He tried to make conversation but I was in so much pain I could hardly move. My ribs were screaming with agony and I knew some of them must be broken. My legs kept buckling underneath me when I tried to walk. Presumably they didn't want to leave me in the field for any passers-by to find, so someone loaded me into the back of a filthy white van. The windows were all boarded up so no one would be able to see me from the outside. Several of them climbed into the front and chatted to one another as if I wasn't there as I rolled around in the dirt of the floor. Every bump the van went over sent spasms of pain shooting through me.

They stopped at the top of the M23 motorway to drop me off. I couldn't see how I could look after myself in the state I was in. I asked them to take me home, but they wouldn't do that, not wanting to get involved any more than they already were. They compromised and offered to drop me off in Coulsdon high street. By then it was late and the streets were more or less empty. As they drove away I half walked and half crawled into a mini-cab office. Everyone stared at me.

'You all right, son?' someone asked.

'Yeah,' I mumbled through broken lips, 'just get me a cab to take me home.'

A car came round immediately and the driver helped me get in. When he dropped me off I paid him out of what I'd earned. I hauled myself upstairs to the bedroom and collapsed on the bed. I just wanted to end it all. I felt I'd tried my best to get started in life, and I just wasn't succeeding. There didn't seem to be any point in going on. But, unless you're going to kill yourself, you can't give up. You have to keep trying. A few days later, once I'd started to mend,

I began to rack my brains for other ways to break out of the destructive cycle of debt and poverty that I'd got myself into.

20

In Pursuit of Quick Cash

Because of the house, my creditors were becoming more and more impatient. I seemed to be receiving summonses almost every day for one unpaid bill or another. Having reached the bottom of the barrel with the bare-knuckle fighting I had two choices as to where I could go next; I could either give up the house and just walk away from the whole mess, or I could keep struggling to achieve my childhood dreams of freedom and prosperity. I decided, once my body had mended enough to support me, to keep trying.

I still wanted to buy the bar and, when I made enquiries, I discovered that it was still for sale. Had I been a more experienced businessman that might have raised some queries in my mind, but I was so desperate to get my hands on it I didn't think too deeply about why no one else had snapped it up after I dropped out. Originally the plan had been for me to pay a £20,000 deposit, and the rest out of the profits the bar produced. The business had done really well in the past but had lost some of its excitement, mainly because the owner had lost interest in it. It's the sort of business where you need to be very hands-on and enthusiastic if you're going to get the right buzz going, otherwise the customers just drift off to the competition. I thought I could revive its reputation quite easily because I was willing to put a great deal of time and effort into it, and I was bubbling with ideas. I had no experience in the industry to base this on, I'd never even worked behind a bar pulling pints. I had no idea how the business worked, apart from supplying dodgy drinks, but I was brimming with confidence that I could pull it off. I'd been planning to use the remaining £10,000 of Margaret's loan to get the stock levels up and do the place up a bit.

I'd been so looking forward to getting started on the venture and had been telling the owner that the money was on its way for a few weeks. Then, when Margaret changed her mind, I'd had to confess to him that I hadn't got the money. It made me sound like an idiot, like some kid who was living in a fantasy world. But I had to keep trying to find another way round, because I really wanted to get into this business, certain that it would give me the foothold I needed to move up in the world and make some solid money. Having pulled myself together, I called him up and we arranged to meet.

'How much can you get?' he wanted to know when I told him I still wanted to make the deal happen if it was at all possible.

'I don't know,' I replied, racking my brain for anyone that I might be able to borrow a bit of money from. 'Give me a few days.'

A few days later I came back, having been to see everyone I knew who might be able to help out. I'd also sold everything I could lay my hands on, even taking the old fridge and washing machine that Margaret had left in the kitchen and selling them to the scrap heap for a few pounds. I went back and told him I could come up with £7,000 if he could give me a couple of weeks. He obviously hadn't had any better offers from anywhere else and he accepted. I would have to make up the difference in payments from the cash flow each week.

I'd managed to raise some of the money by selling things, but I was still five thousand short of the figure I'd promised him, and now I only had two weeks in which to get it. I was going to have to find a quick deal that would earn me a few thousand. It required drastic action. I contacted the South London garage owner who'd been buying the rental cars off Paul and me. It wasn't a contact I wanted to make but I couldn't think of anything else. We arranged to meet.

'I need five grand,' I told him. 'What do you need?

He pulled out a list of cars that he needed. There were ten on the list. 'If you can get me those in the next two weeks,' he said, 'I'll give you five grand, but they've all got to have keys and be ready to go.'

Since I had no contact in a rental company any more, I was going to have to find the cars on the streets, which was a much more frightening prospect than simply dealing with Paul. I didn't like the idea of resorting to crime in order to raise the money, but I could see no other way. It seemed to me that if I didn't raise enough money to get into a legitimate business I was going to go under anyway. I justified it to myself with the belief that once I'd got myself into the bar business I would be able to stay within the law for the rest of my life. There just didn't seem to be any honest way that I could raise the sort of money I needed in order to lead a good, straight life. I was going to have to do this one last illegal thing to give myself a chance to succeed, not go bankrupt and to earn myself some self-respect. My mind was made up, so now I just had to develop an efficient method of working that would minimize the risks of getting caught while I collected the cars I required.

The first thing I needed was a car of my own to cruise around the streets in, and that car had to be totally legal so I wouldn't get pulled over or attract any attention to myself as I moved around. I did still have an old car of my own, so I made sure everything about it was legal and then set out on the search. I was determined that I wasn't going to stop working until I'd completed the list. It was a bit like an illegal treasure hunt. I drove around for hour after hour, my eyes constantly scanning the sides of the roads. When I got too tired I'd park up in a side street and doze in the car, setting off again on the search as soon as I felt refreshed. I ate all my meals at the wheel as I scoured the streets for the exact models and colours my contact had asked for. The cars were mainly Fords and Vauxhalls; anonymous makes that could be sold easily at auctions without attracting undue attention.

Whenever I spotted a car that was on the list I'd make a note of where it was, and of the garage that had supplied it, the name usually being written under the registration number or on a sticker somewhere on the back window. I would then ring the garage, tell them I'd lost my keys, give them the registration number and make of the car and ask them to give me the key number. I'd make my voice sound as desperate as possible: 'Could you please help me? I'm late for the airport and I've dropped my keys down the drain. Please help. I've been told all I need is the key number.'

I didn't want to make the call memorable for them should the police ever come round asking questions about that particular car. It was like acting and I found I was rather good at it. The garages never questioned it, and it's unlikely the police ever thought to contact any of them when the cars were reported stolen anyway. The people who answered my calls never asked for any proof that I was the owner of the car in question, they just gave me the numbers over the phone. Easy as pie. I could never have stolen a car any other way. I had no idea how to put wires together under a bonnet or break a lock. I couldn't have smashed my way through a window or any of the other methods which street crooks use. It wouldn't have been any good if I had, my contact didn't want to buy damaged goods; he wanted pristine cars with keys.

Once I had the numbers I needed I took them to a key-cutting service and they, having no reason to be suspicious, did the job. Once I had the key I would go back to pick the car up. I'd have a pushbike in the back of my car, which I would transfer to the stolen car, so I could get back to my car once I'd delivered the stolen one to a street near to my contact.

When I took the cars I always wore a suit and looked like the sort of person who would be driving whatever car it was. Some of them I found parked around airports, so I even carried a briefcase, which I'd pop into the boot as I picked it up, to make it look more natural and to attract less attention. Who was ever likely to remember seeing a man in a suit putting his briefcase into the back of a car at an airport and then just driving away in it? I must admit I did look a bit silly cycling back to my car in a suit, a rucksack on my back with the briefcase inside. Sometimes the car was too far away to cycle, so I'd take the train or taxi back.

One of the cars I took was a 24-valve Granada. It was a powerful motor and I was driving it a little too fast as I took it away from the scene of the crime, just as someone who owned such a car probably would have done. As I shot through a side street I came head to head with a police car coming in the opposite direction, narrowly missing a collision. I slowed down and watched in my rear-view mirror. To my horror I saw the police car stopping and turning round. It was possible they would just give me a talking to and send me on my way, but it wasn't a chance I was willing to take. I put my foot to the floor and shot away down the back roads, my eyes constantly flicking to the mirror to see if they were in sight, my heart thumping. When I was a few streets from home and hadn't seen them for a while, I parked up, got out and ran back to the house. I slammed and locked the door behind me. Once safely inside I stayed in for the rest of the night, dreading the sound of a knock on the door. In the morning I sauntered back to the car and it was still there. No one seemed to be paying it any undue attention. I must have lost them almost immediately in the back streets of Coulsdon. I climbed back in and finished the delivery.

Often I couldn't deliver the stolen cars to my contact immediately and had to park them up overnight somewhere. If that happened I needed to change the number plates in case someone spotted them. I'd go through a copy of *Exchange and Mart* until I found a similar model of the same age and colour and I'd ring up and ask for the registration number, giving some story about how I needed to check it out before I came to look at it. I'd then get false number plates made up with the number they gave me. I would take the tax disc off so that there was no way a pair of prying eyes could see there wasn't a match. That way I knew the car would be safe until it was collected. I was becoming a real professional.

By working night and day I managed to deliver all ten cars the day before my two-week deadline was up. I'd made it; I had enough money to do the deal. All my plans were now in place: I would buy the bar, get it going and that would give me enough money to cover the mortgage payments and get my life on the right tracks. I phoned my contact in the garage to ask for the money he now owed me.

'I won't be able to get it till next week,' he said.

I felt disappointed. I was eager to get my life moving, but I could understand that he needed to get paid for some of the cars himself, and I thought I could hold the bar deal off for one more week now that I knew the money was coming. I was terrified of losing the deal, but if the garage guy hadn't got the money to give to me I had no choice but to be patient for a little longer. Why did things never go like I hoped? I rang again the following week. I couldn't get hold of him. I kept trying but I was starting to feel uneasy.

'Where's my money?' I asked whenever I got hold of him and he kept putting me off with different excuses.

Eventually he told me he hadn't got it. 'You've got to wait for the cars to be sold,' he said.

'That wasn't the deal,' I insisted. I was beginning to feel like he was making a fool of me. I didn't like having to ring up and plead for money that was rightfully mine. 'The deal was you paid when I got the cars. You always have money. Just pay me what I'm owed.'

I knew this guy always carried around a wad of notes and had more in the safe. There was no way he was completely cleaned out. I could see my only chance to succeed in a real business going down the tubes if I let this man mess me about. I was feeling desperate. Every day I had to wait seemed like an eternity. I knew too many older guys who'd left it too long to get going in a legitimate business, who were always dreaming of what they were going to do and never actually getting it together. I dreaded becoming one of them. I'd been struggling for long enough; I now had to get the ball rolling. I'd worked so hard during that fortnight to get the cars; I'd succeeded and now I was being messed about.

Although everyone thought I was connected to the dangerous guys who ran some of the dodgier clubs and businesses, I'd never actually gone to them and asked for any favours. I'd never needed to, just having my name linked to them was usually enough to make people wary of messing me around. I knew they liked me and would probably oblige, but I'd never wanted to put myself in their debt. I liked the relationship just as it was. These were evil sons-of-bitches but I trusted them and they could trust me; that's how we bonded. I kept my mouth shut and they did whatever they had to do. But now I was desperate and I had to do something significant if I didn't want to end up bankrupt and on the street. I had no choice. I went to see them and told them I needed a gun.

21

Guns and Lay-Bys

Guns and drugs were two things I'd never got involved with. I always believed that cars and alcohol were fairly frivolous crimes compared to these. But if I didn't take significant action now I was going to lose what felt like my last chance.

My contacts didn't ask any questions. They simply agreed to help and I was told the gun would cost £200. I said that would be okay and a meeting was set up in a lay-by at the side of a dual carriageway. I was told the type of car I should look out for. The meeting was scheduled for the next evening and everything happened so quickly and efficiently I barely had time to take it in. My nerves were tight. If I was caught in possession of a gun it would ruin any chances I would ever have of leading a straight life, but I could still see no alternative. The guy was never going to give me my money just because I was asking for it. He had to be shown that I meant business.

It was around nine at night as I drove through the dark towards the spot that had been described to me. I saw the car already there and pulled up in front of it, watching my contact in the rear-view mirror for a few seconds before getting out. He was a tall, stocky man in his late forties, dressed in dark, nondescript clothes. He had his bonnet up and was fiddling around in the engine, pretending something was wrong. I went up to him and said nothing.

'It's by the next lamp-post,' he said, without looking up. 'The poppers are at the one after that.'

With that he pulled down the bonnet support and snapped the lid shut, climbed back into the driving seat and started the engine. He drove off without giving me a second look. I got back into my car and drove on. The road was quiet, just the occasional headlights passing by. My heart was pounding as I tried to see the lamp-post he meant, but there didn't seem to be another one. My stomach was cramping up and the palms of my hands were sweating on the wheel. Then I realized I'd passed it. I had to go back. Every nerve in my body was tight with fear. This was like nothing I'd ever done before. This seemed like serious danger. When I finally got to the place there was a folded black plastic sack lying in the dark at the base of the post. I didn't stop to look inside. It could have contained a dead cat for all I knew, I just wanted to get out of there. I chucked it on to the floor in the back of the car and drove off. I didn't bother to stop for the bullets. I had no intention of killing anyone, or of getting killed myself. As long as I didn't have any ammunition that was less likely to happen. I didn't even need to know if the gun worked, as long as it looked as if it did. This was going to be a game of bluff.

I felt more scared than I had since I was a child as I drove with the bag on the floor behind me. Everything that had happened to me in the previous months had been piling more and more stress on to me, and now I'd reached a point where I was driving about in the middle of the night with a gun in the car. I felt physically sick, but determined to go through with it. I couldn't afford to show weakness now or I'd be finished; I'd never get my money and without the money I wouldn't get the bar and I'd lose the house and end up on the streets. I had to keep going. My first thought was that if I got caught and sent to prison, at least I'd have a room of my own to sleep in, which I soon wouldn't have on the outside if I didn't raise the money. It was all driving me to madness.

When I got back home I went out into the garden, right to the far end, carrying the unopened bag. Everything was silent and black as I scrambled under the fence to one of the neighbours' houses, burrowing beneath their compost heap and pushing the bag deep inside the hole. The rich smell of the steaming, rotted compost filled the night air. I knew they didn't have a dog, so nothing would disturb my hiding place. I straightened up the fence again. At least now the weapon wasn't on my premises and I had time to breathe and think what to do next.

When I got back into the house, all my muscles still shaking with fear, I realized I hadn't eaten all day, my stomach had been feeling too tight with nerves to be able to handle food. I left the silent, empty house and went down to the fish and chip shop, ordering double portions of everything, bringing it back to the house and scoffing it all down as fast as I could get it into my mouth, desperate to fill my stomach and deaden the hunger pains. As I pushed the last mouthful in I sank down into the chair, my stomach now uncomfortably distended, although my hunger had been sated. Every inch of me felt full. An hour later I was kneeling in the bathroom with my fingers down my throat, bringing back every last morsel of the meal, trying to lose the uncomfortable, unhealthy feeling of being stuffed. It was the first time I'd ever done such a thing, but it wouldn't be the last.

I knew I had to act fast. Firstly I didn't want the gun around for a moment longer than necessary and secondly I needed the money to do the deal. Once I'd calmed down, and dozed a little, I went outside to bring the gun back in before dawn broke. I didn't want to be seen rummaging around in someone else's compost heap in the daylight. I brought the bag back into the house and opened it. This was the first time I'd studied the weapon. It was heavy and cumbersome. It looked like something from an old World War Two movie. I stood in front of the mirror in the bathroom and practised holding it up.

'Just give me my money,' I said, but my voice was trembling. I took a deep breath and focused my mind. 'Just give me my money,' I said again.

I had to be sure my hand wouldn't shake at the critical moment. He had to believe I was completely calm and in control. I wanted to look like someone who was used to handling firearms. If he saw me shaking he'd know I was bluffing. He had to believe I was willing and able to pull the trigger if I didn't get what I wanted. I practised for a while, getting used to the feel of it, waiting for daylight and a time when I knew my contact would be in his garage. I was going to wear a glove on my right hand. It had to be a big glove, so I could slip it on and off my hand easily. I didn't want to draw attention to myself by being seen to be wearing gloves in spring on the way in or out of the garage. The problem was, I could hardly fit my finger round the trigger when I had it on. I practised until I had a technique that worked.

As it grew lighter outside I dressed myself very carefully

in a blue suit and shirt. I wanted to look relaxed but smart. I didn't want to look desperate. I went back to the mirror and held the gun up again.

'Just give me my money,' I repeated for the hundredth time. I was surprised by how confident I looked.

I didn't have a holster so I had to work out how to carry it so that it wouldn't be noticed by anyone else and wouldn't fall out. In the end the only place was the inside pocket of my jacket. It was far too big and I had to walk with my arm clenched across my chest to hold it in, but it was the only option.

My target operated from a scruffy little garage, opening on to a South London high street. There were no customers around as I came in, just a mechanic working under the bonnet of one of the cars. As I pushed the door to the office behind me I turned the 'open' sign to 'closed'. There were people passing by outside on their way to work or the shops, unaware of the tense scene going on a few feet away from them. Seeing me, and knowing I'd want to talk business, the owner came out of the office and told the mechanic to close the gates that the cars came in through at the back. I guess he thought we were going to have an argument. Perhaps he even planned to teach me a lesson for being so pushy.

As soon as the gates were shut I pulled out the gun and pointed it at him, turning my back to the window so passers-by wouldn't see anything. He was shocked. I thought my hand was shaking, but if it was, he didn't notice. He backed off immediately, his whole tone changing.

'Just give me my money!' I said.

All the rehearsals had paid off. The words came out with all the controlled menace I'd hoped for. I realized that the man in front of me, who I'd thought of as a real hard nut, was now shitting himself, shaking, backing off and apologizing, trying to make light of the whole situation. If only he'd known just how scared I was inside. If only he'd known the gun was as harmless as a child's toy.

'You,' I said to the mechanic, who was standing, staring with his mouth hanging open, 'fuck off!' And he scurried away.

I knew they weren't going to be calling the police because I could see they still had some of my cars sitting around the premises.

'I just want my money,' I said.

'I haven't got it.' He spread his hands as if helpless to do anything about the situation.

'Either you've got it,' I said, lifting the gun as if taking aim at his head, 'or you're going.'

I needed him to believe I was mad enough to kill someone for five thousand pounds. In fact, if I'd had bullets and he'd refused to pay it's possible I would have shot him. I had nothing to lose by that stage and I might well have turned the gun on myself afterwards.

'Okay, okay, okay!' He held his hands up to slow me down. 'Calm down, calm down.' It looked like I'd convinced him but there was still time for him to double-cross me again.

He walked to the safe, jabbering nervously all the way, and opened it. As the door of the safe swung back I couldn't believe my eyes. I'd never seen so much money in my life. Every deal he ever did must have been for cash and he can't ever have been near a bank. It was crammed with piles of money, all wrapped in neat packages. I was now really angry. If I'd had bullets I might have started firing.

'Why the fuck didn't you pay me?' I shouted, gesturing at the safe with the gun. 'You had all that and you couldn't give me the few thousand you owed!'

'It's just business,' he shrugged. 'Just take the money.'

He must have been able to see how serious I was because he was shaking and sweating uncontrollably. There must have been a hundred thousand or more in the safe and I could have walked out with it all, but I knew that would lead to more trouble. This way he might have lost a bit of face, but he would only have paid me what I was owed. If I'd stolen from him he might have hired someone to come after me. I would always be having to look over my shoulder and that was exactly what I was hoping to get away from by buying into a legitimate business. This way it was a fair deal. I'd already learnt that it was sometimes the smallest people who could cause you the most trouble if you upset them.

'I only want what you owe me,' I said. 'Give me my five thousand and two hundred for collection expenses.'

I didn't see why I should have to pay for the loan of the gun. It didn't occur to me to take any more than I was owed. The rest wasn't my money and I hadn't earned it. I wanted to get a reputation for being someone you didn't cheat, not as someone who went round robbing people.

He pulled the right amount of money out in bundles of twenty pound notes, each bundle worth a thousand pounds. The hardest part was waiting while he counted out the two hundred pounds. It seemed to take an eternity. Having got my money I put the gun away and turned to leave the premises. Once outside, a smile slowly came to my face as I realized I was on my way to having my own legitimate business. I felt good about having taken charge of the situation and got my money. Now I had to get rid of the gun as soon as possible.

As I drove away a tear ran down my cheek. I guess it was pure happiness, but maybe it was also because of what I'd been reduced to doing just in order to get what was owing to me. Now I could live again.

Once I was back at the house I scrubbed the gun clean of fingerprints, wearing gloves to handle it from then on. I put it in a bin bag, being careful to get no prints on the plastic, then put that bag into another so I could carry it. I burned all the gloves on the bonfire, which I kept at the bottom of the garden. I made a phone call to my contacts to say I was returning the gun to where I'd found it and went out to the car, driving to the same lay-by. When I got to the lamp-post I did the same thing as the man who'd dropped it there, making a big thing about putting the bonnet of the car up, so that I'd have an alibi if anyone happened to spot me. I prayed no police would draw up to ask me what was wrong. I walked casually to the lamp-post and tipped the inner bag out of the outer one, putting the outer one back in the car to take home to burn. I didn't want anyone ever to be able to trace that weapon back to me.

A week later I bought the bar and from that moment I noticed that people looked at me differently wherever I went. I'd suddenly become 'someone', just because I owned a bar. Word gets around quickly about something like that. A lot of people started offering me drinks out of respect, but I never accepted. I didn't want to owe anyone anything.

22

The Bar Business

So 'The Kid' had moved into the bar business. I knew the place already as I'd been going there as a customer, although it wasn't a place I ever did business with when I was selling drink. It was always busy but it had gone downhill and needed a new set of hands at the wheel. I was twenty-two years old and knew nothing about the business, I'd never worked in any bar before and my only contact was that sometimes I supplied other bars and clubs with drink. But none of this bothered me. I was quietly confident in my ability to succeed. I'd managed to get this far against the odds, hadn't I?

On my first evening there I was really nervous but knew I couldn't show it. I needed to show everyone that I was in charge or I would be ripped off left, right and centre. I'd gone in the previous day and been shown the technical ins and outs of the place like how the alarm worked, the safe, the computer system which controlled the tills and stock and how to change a barrel, all the usual things that go on when handing over a business. The one thing I wasn't shown was how to pull a pint. But it didn't matter as I wasn't planning to serve behind the bar on the first night. I kept a close eye on the girls to see how they did it. The evening went well and I began to feel even more confident. Everyone treated me with the respect you would expect of a boss. That night I stayed behind after closing time and practised until I could pour a perfect pint. I was now ready to serve my customers with confidence as well as enthusiasm.

The place had great potential. There were two DJ stands, two bars, and a huge television screen up on the wall but, best of all, I was the youngest man on the premises. I didn't allow anyone in who was under twenty-five years old because I knew it was the older punters who had the money to spend. I didn't want loads of teenagers filling the place up and buying one drink an evening. I wasn't even old enough or experienced enough to hold a licence, so I employed the previous manager to help run it, to be a licensee and be my second man.

I was already known by the staff before I arrived and they seemed as keen as me to make a fresh start and give the place a new lease of life. Everything in my life changed overnight. At first business was slow. We were less than half full and the customers weren't coming in before nine at night to have a drink before they went clubbing. I made a drastic decision and decided to take a gamble. I believed that in order to get people through the door I needed outside help. I was running a cool bar so I decided to have a celebrity DJ on Friday nights. I hired Neil Fox from Capital Radio. He came in once or twice a month and would mention us on his radio show, saying where he was going. We put banners outside the bar and word got round quickly. The first night he came we had queues outside the bar from seven in the evening and we had to call the bouncers to come in early to control them. The bar was back to its former glory in no time and I was sure I had a flair for the business, which would take me right to the top.

Money was pouring into the tills and every night seemed to be party night. On a Friday I'd be standing on the bar tipping tequila down people's throats. Bank holidays would be theme nights with all the staff dressing up, which pleased the lads greatly. I even put in a dental chair, which customers sat in while I poured the tequila into them. The place had a great buzz. Fridays would be club night so the music was modern and got everyone in the mood for a great night out. It was also girls' and lads' night out. On Saturdays it was mostly couples who came into the bar, although they were often the same people who'd been in the night before without their partners. Sunday was 70s and 80s night and was always packed. It felt as if I had finally arrived.

There was never any trouble because the rumour had gone around that I wasn't someone you messed about with. I did nothing to dispel the rumours; none of it served me badly. People knew not to cause trouble in my bar. Me, I was just happy, smiling, joking and really enjoying my job.

Money was rolling in and my first job was to keep up to date with my current mortgage payments. That kept the mortgage company at bay, although they were still after the back payments. I went to court a couple of times because they wanted to repossess the house, but the judge knew I was trying my best and gave me time to get myself on my feet so long as I could keep up the current payments.

Each week I met the previous owner of the bar to go through the accounts and he would get what he was due, but it seemed that each week, as we were making more and more, he also wanted more and more. He didn't get away with it all the time but I could tell he was envious of how I'd brought the bar back from the brink.

A meeting was booked to see the brewery that had

supplied the bar before I took over. I thought nothing of it, assuming they were going to show me their beers. The local rep came in and introduced himself. He asked a few questions and I told him that I'd bought the bar, paying a deposit and buying the rest of it through the takings of the business.

'Strange,' he said. 'I can't see how. You see, the man you "bought" it off owes the brewery over £350,000 and we have a charge on this property. We're looking to foreclose on him.'

My mouth must have dropped six inches. I couldn't believe what I was hearing. Because of my inexperience and eagerness and because I was so desperate to get a foothold in a legitimate business, I'd signed the contract that the previous owner had put in front of me without really reading it. It was my own fault, but I'd let him take advantage of my naivety. I was mad but I knew I had to bide my time if I wanted to salvage anything from the wreckage. My dreams had been shattered once more. I might be enjoying the job, but I wasn't building a business I could do anything with.

I managed to keep the place afloat on cash flow for about nine months and then I realized I couldn't do it any longer. The previous owner had debts everywhere and all I was really being was a glorified manager. I'd been ripped off. I'd poured the money in and taken hardly anything out, but in fact I'd never owned anything worth having. In the end I realized I was out of my depth. There was nothing I could do to straighten the situation out. So I made a conscious decision to leave. I took what money there was in the safe – about three grand – and left the keys with the manager, who I asked to inform the previous owner of my decision.

When he found out he started calling me and issuing threats, saying he wanted the rest of his money, but I took no notice. I had bigger problems than him on my plate.

Once I was out of the bar I had a lot of time on my hands to think over my situation, and I realized just how badly he'd ripped me off with the whole deal. The suppliers were now after me for unpaid bills. Because I'd kept paying them regularly there was only about £13,000 in all. I heard that the bar owner was going around telling people I was a 'nobody' and that he'd 'dealt with me'. After about a week I decided I had to do something about it. I called him.

'I want my original seven grand back,' I told him. I thought that if I got that back I wouldn't feel so bad and could pay some of my creditors off. But also after going to so much trouble to raise the seven grand I felt I deserved to keep it. 'I'm coming round for it.'

He simply laughed and hung up the phone. He fancied himself as being a bit tough, just because he was in the bar business, but I knew better. I needed help so I put a call in to my former contacts, the ones who had got me the gun, explaining what had happened. They knew I had the bar, having wished me all the best when I started. It was out of their area so they weren't bothered by the competition. They asked me for his telephone number and said they'd give him a call. Half an hour later the bar owner was back on the phone to me, oozing jollity and friendliness and suggesting we meet up to sort things out. It seemed that one phone call from my friends had been enough to change his whole attitude.

'It needs to be a neutral place,' he said, obviously worried about the call he'd just received. 'And we need someone else there.' He suggested the name of a mutual friend who'd first introduced the two of us.

The three of us met in a pub car park a couple of hours later. He was waiting in the back of a car for me. I got in beside him and ignored his outstretched hand of friendship.

'You fucked me over,' I said, 'I ought to pop you here and now.'

He wasn't to know that I never wanted to see another gun as long as I lived. I think the rumours about what I'd done in the past had finally reached him and he seemed to take this threat seriously.

'Of course,' he said, all smiles and reasonableness, 'none of this is personal. It's only business.'

I was sick of hearing that line from people who thought that cheating people was fair as long as it could be called business.

'This is what is going to happen,' I went on. 'You're going to take over the thirteen grand debt and I'm going to keep the money from the safe.'

I knew that doing it this way would completely clear my business debts and I would then be able to focus on what I was going to do next, concentrating my efforts on clearing the personal debts which were still hanging over me since the purchase of the house.

He agreed to take over the debts and I was now free of the bar, but still not free of debt. I had to come up with another way to generate money, quickly, if I wasn't to end up back where I started. Those nine months in the bar had given me a taste for running my own place. I went to see one of the breweries to ask if they would give me somewhere, but I was still too young, only just turning twenty-three, and didn't have enough experience for their tastes.

The one thing I learnt out of the whole experience was how few real friends anyone has. Alan had always told me that you could count your true friends on the fingers of one hand and I could now see that he was right. As long as I was a bar owner I seemed to have hundreds of friends, but when the bar went, so did they. The ones who stuck by me knew me before the bar and were friends because of me, not because of my job.

23

Living on the Edge

The night that I threw up my fish and chips proved not to be an isolated incident. My bulimia was growing worse. Most people think it's a complaint that only strikes women; they're wrong. Because I was so desperate to succeed and keep my head above water I had to bottle up all my worries and nerves in order to appear cool. Whether I was posing as a hard man with a gun, quelling my anxieties about stealing cars, or trying to keep afloat a bar that was already weighed down with debt, the pressures were enormous for someone who had no one to confide in. I was constantly on edge inside my own head. I would eat far too much, just in order to comfort myself and banish all telltale signs of hunger that might remind me of the horrors of my child-hood. Feeling guilty and uncomfortable, I would then bring it back up soon after. Perhaps my subconscious always remembered those early years of hunger at home, and warned me to eat as much as possible while I could, because it might end at any moment. Late at night, when all the stresses and worries seemed to pile up, I'd stuff myself on chocolate, going on and on until I felt gorged, and then I'd go into the bathroom and purge myself, wanting to feel clean again. It was a sad and solitary way of existing.

As I sat in the once homely house, which was pulling me further and further into debt, staring at the worn bits of carpet on the floor for hours on end, trying to work out where I kept going wrong, it felt as if I was more or less back where I'd started. The slump in the property market was still going on and the house was now worth less than the mortgage I had on it. If I sold it I'd still be in debt to the building society for the difference. I was still spending Christmases alone, still buying my own birthday presents, still struggling to find a way to get rid of the debts, let alone build some capital to make my dreams come true. All I wanted from life was a chance to get started, to get on the first rung of the ladder, but no one seemed ready to give it to me. People I did business with tried to rip me off and nobody would give me an honest chance to prove my abilities. I felt that I was still trapped in a tiny room with no doors, just as I had been when I was a child. I was tired, tired of the mistakes I'd made, tired of the choices I'd made, tired of the constant struggle since childhood; but most of all I was tired of being alone. I had no more energy for the fight.

24

The End of the Road

I'd never been scared of death, so I decided to end my life. There just didn't seem to be any point in going on.

The process of taking my own life started in the most mundane of ways, with a shopping trip down to the high street. I went to two different chemists' shops and bought two large boxes of paracetamol. I knew if I tried to buy them both at the same place it might arouse the suspicions of the people behind the counter. My favourite drink was Jack Daniel's, so I bought myself a bottle to help wash the tablets down.

I'd weighed up the various possibilities open to me. I'd thought about sitting in the car in the garage with a pipe from the exhaust to the window, but it seemed an unpleasant and dirty way to die. I thought about falling into the Thames, but someone might see me and try to save me. I didn't want to attract attention. I imagined that with tablets I'd just fall asleep and be taken away from here. It seemed the neatest and easiest way to go.

I walked slowly back home with my shopping. There didn't seem to be any reason to hurry, since I only had one thing left to do. I locked the heavy Victorian front door behind me and then deadlocked it. No one else had keys to the house, but I didn't want to take any chances. I'd been shocked by how quickly all the friends I'd had when I was the owner of a popular bar had disappeared the moment I went back to just being myself. I suppose they were all only acquaintances, not real friends.

What I was about to do was not a cry for help; I didn't want to be found until I had gone, this was a decision to end everything. I got myself a glass of water, went up to the bedroom and locked that door from the inside as well.

A guy called Peter had turned up unannounced one day. He'd lived at the house with Margaret when he was a kid and I think he imagined she was still there. I could see he was upset and invited him in. It must have been a shock for him to see the place that once seemed so homely and lived-in looking so desolate. He was in a terrible state. His girlfriend had left him, he'd lost his job and he was deep in debt. He seemed to be close to killing himself. This was before I got the money for the bar and all I had was about a hundred quid in my pocket. I felt so sorry for him, so I gave it to him. I felt really good about being able to do something for someone else. Now I knew how he felt.

I had a small hi-fi in the room and I put on a classical CD which I'd discovered in a shop and which had some of the tunes Colin Smith had recorded for me all those years ago, including 'Ebben? Ne andrò lontana' which had had such an effect on me. Instead of accompanying me on my dream trip to America, as I had once imagined it would, it was going to provide a background for a different sort of journey. The familiar music was soothing and provided me with a little company as I prepared myself for my last few minutes. I left the curtains open, I didn't want the neighbours noticing closed curtains and calling the police.

I sat down on the bed and swallowed a handful of tablets, washed down by swigs of Jack Daniel's. A few minutes later I was in the bathroom, spewing them up. That was obviously not the way to do it. I decided to forget the Jack Daniel's and swallow the rest of the tablets with plain water. I went back into the bedroom and started again, swallowing so many tablets it started to hurt in my chest where the sharp edges had dug in on their way down to my stomach. When the tablets had all gone I lay down on the bed and felt a sleepiness creeping over me as my body finally started to relax and my mind seemed to float away. I was aware that I was falling into a deep sleep. Tears were running silently down my cheeks. It had all been so disappointing, but now I was going and I didn't have to worry or struggle any more. It felt like the most enormous relief.

25

Waking Up

I could see the ceiling of the room moving slowly around above me. I was terribly thirsty. In my confusion I thought I was in a new place but as my mind cleared I realized I'd actually just come round from what was no more than an overdose. I wasn't dead. The tablets hadn't been enough to finish me off, but they'd left me unable to move or even think straight. I lay motionless for what seemed like an eternity, too drowsy and lethargic to make a move, just as I had felt on the way into this big sleep.

I must have slept for a couple of days. I had no idea what day of the week it was when I'd lain down, so I couldn't tell how much time had passed when I woke up. I'd never been a great sleeper; I could never lie in bed in the mornings, right from the days when I used to go out searching the streets for milk floats. Once I was awake I had to get up. But this was different. I guess my body was exhausted and needed the sleep that the tablets allowed. The thirst was becoming unbearable. I was going to have to do something to relieve it. With an enormous effort I pulled my body up into a sitting position. I waited for the room to stop spinning enough to be able to stand without falling and hauled myself off the bed. After a momentary wobble I managed to find my balance and walked slowly to the door, carefully placing each foot in front of the other. It was hard to get my thoughts together enough to unlock the bedroom door. I was still too drugged, lethargic and exhausted to be able to work out how to turn a key. I had virtually no strength left as I plodded downstairs in search of water.

Once I'd satisfied my thirst I crawled back on to the bed and drifted in and out of sleep for a few more hours. During my periods of wakefulness I started to assess the situation. If I wasn't dead, I was going to have to take some very definite steps about getting my life on track. Things suddenly seemed clearer and less hopeless. Perhaps all I'd needed was a complete rest, which I'd given myself by accident. It was time to see things more objectively and positively. Now perhaps I'd be able to find the energy to start the fight all over again, wiping the slate clean and going after the dreams I'd lived for as a child. I lay thinking about America and the ideas I'd had about getting there one day and finding freedom and happiness. I remembered how passionately I'd wanted to be a futures trader and how I'd somehow lost my direction in the hustle and bustle of trying to survive and trying to get together the capital I was still certain would be my passport to success.

'Okay,' I thought to myself. 'You've been given another chance, this time you're not going to waste it.'

I stayed behind that locked front door for about a week, getting my strength together and recovering from the pills. It was a good rest and I began to see things more clearly.

I made a list of my true friends; people who'd stuck by me through the ups and downs. One by one I called them, when my strength had returned, pretending nothing had happened and being my usual upbeat self, seeing how they were getting on and talking like guys do.

I was now ready to restart the upward struggle.

26

Starting Again

The first thing I did was swallow my pride and sign on for unemployment benefit. I'd never wanted to go that route because I'd seen how it had degraded Gloria, and the rest of us through her. I didn't want to be the sort of person who had to rely on the state for support because I wasn't able to stand on my own feet. It had always seemed to me that the weekly Giro had been part of our problem in the past rather than part of the solution. I wanted to be independent of any state assistance. But now it was time to be practical. They would give me some cash so I could eat and get myself back on the road again. To my amazement, when I went in to see them and gave them my details, I discovered they would also pay my mortgage for me. That bought me a little more time.

A few weeks later a friend told me he knew of a couple of guys who wanted to rent a room. Would I be interested? I would have done this before if I hadn't been afraid of the house being repossessed. It hadn't seemed like an option. Also, I was wheeling and dealing at the time and I didn't want other people around the house. I needed privacy and security. It was all nonsense, of course, which I now saw very clearly.

The two guys moved in and within a couple of weeks, with the rent money coming in, I was able to sign off from unemployment benefits. I immediately felt far better. I started to get back into the swing of life. With a bit of cash in my pocket from the rent I was able to put together some better deals, buying and selling again as I had been before the bar business.

One evening, sitting in a club with some acquaintances, I spotted a blonde girl across the other side of the dance floor with a bunch of friends. She was really gorgeous. Our eyes met, like in all the clichés you ever heard about boys meeting girls. It was the sort of scene that happens in pubs and clubs around the world every second of the day, a boy sees a girl across the floor and likes the look of her. It was a cliché, but no less exciting for that. I was still desperately shy around women, particularly after the behaviour I'd seen going on at the bar. But this time I knew I had to pluck up the courage to act. I couldn't take the risk of the evening going by and not having made contact with her. If she left without me getting a phone number I might never see her again. It sounds so corny but even before I'd spoken to her I knew this was someone special.

I watched her from the corner of my eye as I tried to act naturally with my friends. I was trying to pluck up the courage to walk across the room and ask her to dance, but I couldn't face the thought of her saying no. It might be she didn't want to dance, or didn't want to leave the table with her friends, and then I would have blown my chance, and it would be a long walk back across the club floor with my wounded pride. Then I saw her get up and go towards the toilets. She walked past our table and I said something to her. She turned and smiled and said something back, then walked on. With my heart in my mouth I stood up and followed her out. I'd committed myself now. I had to go through with it. At least if she said no out here I wouldn't be humiliated in front of the whole club. We chatted for a while and exchanged phone numbers. We stood talking for some time and, amongst other things, I found out her name was Jackie; she was working as a PA, and wasn't in any steady relationship.

She told me she was going away for the weekend so I didn't phone her until Monday and then made the call and asked her out. She agreed. We had a date and I knew at that moment I'd found my soul mate, a best friend and someone I wanted to share the rest of my life with. What had started out as the cliché of a boy spotting a girl he fancies across a crowded bar had blossomed into another cliché; I had fallen hopelessly in love. I couldn't believe how nice she was; as well as beautiful and sexy she was kind and peaceful. It amazed me that she was so beautiful and natural. When we were together she never asked me difficult questions about my past or my situation, just accepted me for what I was and who I was. As the relationship progressed we remained good friends as well as lovers. I was still suffering from bulimia, but I managed to hide that from her. We laughed all the time we were together. I'd never met anyone like her in my life and she changed everything.

Jackie's family was very different to mine. Although her parents were divorced they were both good, kind people who'd brought her up as they should. They were a million miles from Gloria and Dennis and accepted me without a moment's hesitation. They obviously trusted their daughter's judgement. If I was all right by Jackie, that was enough for them.

Suddenly being in such a serious relationship taught me a lot about myself, even trivial things. I hadn't realized quite how fast and greedily I ate my food until I went out for meals with Jackie and had finished whole courses when she was still on her third mouthful. It must have stemmed from the years when Wayne and I would cram food in as quickly as possible, swallowing it without chewing, terrified that someone would catch us and take it away if we didn't hurry. The way I ate must also have contributed to the bloated and uncomfortable feelings I experienced after every meal, which prompted me to make myself sick.

These sorts of things Jackie could point out to me and we could make a joke of them, but there were other aspects of my behaviour which she found too difficult to discuss with me. Three months into the relationship she rang up and said she didn't want to go out with me any more. I couldn't understand it. It had been going so well. How could she want to end it so suddenly? It was a crushing blow.

'Okay,' I said, not wanting to show how devastated I was by this news, and having no idea how to ask her why she'd made such a drastic decision.

For a week I lived with the agony of thinking I'd lost the one person I really wanted, knowing I'd never meet anyone like that again. The relationship had fulfilled all my worst fears of rejection and disappointment. Yet again I'd been shown just how great life could be, and then had the joy snatched away from me. At the end of the week I realized I couldn't just accept it. I had to find out what had made her make such a terrible decision. I rang and asked what I'd done wrong.

'You never show me any affection,' she explained. 'If we're walking down the street you don't walk with me or hold my hand, you just stride on ahead with me following behind. I've really fallen in love with you, Kevin, but you don't show me any sign that you love me.'

As she told me these things, I realized they were true. It was the way I was and I'd thought nothing about it. Now she pointed it out I knew she was right. This was the first true, adult relationship I'd ever had with anyone. I had no experience to draw on as to how to do it. I'd never seen my parents being affectionate to one another and although Alan and Margaret had a good marriage they were not in the first flush of romantic youth when I met them. I found it impossible to show affection. If a child has been rejected by both his parents I guess some shutters are bound to come down somewhere deep inside his brain, to guard him against pain in the future. I couldn't find any way to lift those shutters, however much I wanted to. I was also unreasonably jealous. I was so terrified of losing Jackie now that I'd found her. If she went out for the night with some of her girlfriends, I'd be imagining the sort of goings-on that I'd witnessed during my time in the bar. Even though I knew she wasn't like that, and I trusted her, I couldn't get the pictures out of my mind. Nothing this good had ever happened to me before and I couldn't bear the thought that I might lose it.

By talking about some of the things I'd always kept hidden inside, although never about my childhood, Jackie freed me and I was able to tell her how much I loved her and how I wanted to spend the rest of my life with her. I couldn't believe I'd nearly lost her through pure ignorance. Whenever people see what I've got now and tell me I'm 'lucky', I always think they're wrong. They don't know what I had to go through to get here. I now believe that you have to make your own luck; you have to work hard and if there is something in your life you don't like you have to change it. But if there is one bit of luck I have had, that I will always be grateful for, it was finding Jackie. As soon as she was in my life everything turned round. It didn't happen immediately, but things just kept on getting better.

I started looking for normal jobs again, so I could get the house a bit straight for Jackie, in the hope that she would move in on a permanent basis. I saw an ad for people to sell photocopiers, an industry I had some experience of, and I went for an interview. The company was based in Bow, in East London. I knew I was good at selling and they wanted to pay commission so they were happy to have anyone who would bring in business. I didn't think I was likely to get a better offer from anyone else for a while, given my track record so far, but I gave them one stipulation before I started.

'I'll work hard for you and I'll make you money,' I said, 'but never fuck me with my wages. If I've earned the commission then pay me; never, never mess me about. If it's owed, it's owed.'

I was back on the road and I was making sales. Bit by bit things started to click into place. I straightened out the mortgage so there was no danger of losing the house. I was able to get the lodgers out so Jackie could move in and we could have a nice first home, which we slowly did up and furnished as we could afford it.

Despite the warning I'd issued at my interview, the company I was working for started messing about with my money, just as they all do; not paying me what I was due. I didn't make a big fuss to start with, just nagged them to pay me whenever there was a chance.

27

The Self-Destruct Button

Once we'd overcome our initial difficulties, my relationship with Jackie was going so well I could hardly believe my luck. We seemed to be perfectly in tune about everything. One of the things we were a hundred per cent in agreement over was that we both wanted to have children. There was no great rush, since we were both still young, but we didn't take any birth control precautions, allowing nature to take its course. I'd always thought I could be a great dad. I'd seen so many examples of how not to do it over the years, I felt sure I would be able to learn from my experiences and give my own children everything I never had, both materially and emotionally. I suspect I was also looking forward to having another chance to experience childhood for myself, properly this time.

When Jackie told me she'd fallen pregnant I was beside myself with excitement and delight, hardly able to bear the long months of waiting before we would actually have the baby in the house. I'd been dreaming of the joy of fatherhood for so long. We were both euphoric and felt that something very special was being given to us. After a couple of months, however, when I actually saw the tiny bump swelling in Jackie's stomach I felt a terrible chill of fear. Demons began to appear in my mind, keeping me awake in the small hours of the morning, pricking me with worries and anxieties I hadn't experienced before, bringing me out in a cold sweat. How would I cope with being a father? Would I turn out to be like my own parents? How would I know how to do the right things when they were never done for me? I'd heard so often about how people who abuse children have nearly always been abused themselves. What if I followed the same pattern and found it impossible to control my temper with the child, or was unable to hold myself back from hitting them? Would I, like my parents, turn into an uncontrollable, spiteful, hateful father? If that happened I wouldn't be able to face it.

Ninety-nine per cent of me wanted a child more than anything else in the world, but one per cent was terrified of what would happen to me if I became a parent. As the days passed the one per cent gained a stronger and stronger hold over my mind. I knew I could be a great father, but the negative thoughts were eating away at me, driving me inside my own head and further from Jackie. I couldn't confide my fears to her because I would never have been able to find the words to explain what had happened to me in the past to make me think that I could become a monster. So I started to withdraw from her, throwing myself into my work and staying out late with friends rather than going home and facing my demons. I was drinking more and more, usually Jack Daniel's. I loved Jackie more than anything or anyone and I hated myself for not being able to explain to her what was wrong, but I knew I couldn't tell her about my past. I wanted to explain everything to her but I was so ashamed I couldn't find the words.

Jackie was obviously puzzled and confused by my behaviour, but if she asked me what was wrong I would just reply 'nothing' and retreat even further inside my scrambled head, becoming ever more distant. Jackie is a totally non-argumentative person so she never forced the issue. She took to going round to her mother's more, rather than being alone in the house, waiting for me to come home. It was getting so that we were only seeing one another at weekends. She was becoming increasingly upset which made me angrier with myself for what I was doing to her. She couldn't understand why I was behaving so oddly when she knew that I wanted a child as much as she did. She could see no reason why our wonderful relationship seemed to be suddenly turning so bad.

The tension was growing all around and my bulimia, which had become less acute since I'd been in the relationship, flared up. I was vomiting after almost every meal, something else I was hiding from Jackie, not wanting to face the truth and see the reaction in her eyes. I kept getting flashbacks from parts of my childhood that I'd been successfully suppressing for years, making the nights even more restless and my fears even more ferocious.

I was becoming more and more distant from Jackie and from life in general. I would never want to hurt any child and the thought that I might do so was driving me insane. I was fighting myself and driving away the one person I loved more than anything, but I didn't seem to be able to do anything about it.

One night, while having drinks with some friends, I must have downed the best part of a bottle of Jack Daniel's. A girl I knew a little showed me some affection and I took the bait. I could make all sorts of excuses, like having drunk too much or being under pressure, but none of them would mean anything. It was the worst thing I had ever done and there was no excuse. There was no one else to blame. I could have said no and I didn't. Alan once joked, 'A truly strong man is one who can walk away from a naked woman.' I'd been weak and I was so ashamed I didn't know what to do with myself.

The moment it was over I thought of Jackie and my stomach felt like a thousand butterflies were trying to escape. I knew I had done something terribly wrong and I was disgusted with myself. I was so filled with self-hate I couldn't even look at my face in a mirror. I'd become the sort of man I most despised.

The guilt landed on me so heavily I knew I would never be able to bear it. My love for Jackie was so great I could never lie to her. I'd been fighting with myself for what seemed like an eternity. We wanted each other so much but my behaviour was unacceptable and I couldn't face up to the demons inside. I felt trapped.

I would have to do something or it would crush us both. I deserved to be punished. I realized that I was going to have to confess to Jackie what I'd done if I wanted our relationship to stand any chance of survival. I couldn't hope to spend the rest of my life with her and bring up children together if I'd lied to her about anything. I knew it was going to be a cruel thing to do, but I'd already done the worst thing possible, and to keep it a secret would only be compounding the crime. I might not have told her about my past, but I'd never lied to her and I knew I never could. I had to take control of the situation and face the consequences, even though I was more frightened of losing her than anything else.

I looked deep inside myself and decided the demons were only a small part of me. I was a better man than this. I could be a good husband and father, but not if I didn't deal with the situation as honestly as possible. I told Jackie what I'd done.

Seeing her tears broke my heart. I loved her so much and I was so desperate to spend my life with her and with our child, and now I'd put the whole thing in jeopardy through sheer stupidity and weakness. She obviously wanted to get away from me and went back to stay with her mother.

I realized completely how badly I'd treated her and how much danger I was in; that I might lose everything and end up without Jackie and my child. I was going to have to do everything possible to convince her that I loved her. I had to make her realize how much I missed her when she wasn't there. I had to overcome my fears about how I might react to the baby. Even though we were living under different roofs, I made sure that I went with her to all the pregnancy and childbirth appointments. I put every ounce of effort I could muster into showing Jackie how much I regretted my stupid mistake and how much I wanted to become the best father in the world and to take care of her and our child. I wanted her to know how hard I was willing to work to make our relationship good once more.

Bit by bit the atmosphere improved. She was incredibly forgiving. I would never have been able to forgive such a betrayal if it had been her who had slipped up. She was the only woman I had ever met that I wasn't nervous of. If she had betrayed me I would never have been able to recover. But she was stronger than me, and as we carefully reconstructed our relationship it actually seemed to move on to another level. The sight of Jackie carrying our unborn child was now bringing us so close that it was as if we were inside each other's souls. Our love and Jackie's forgiveness made me see what an incredible, caring woman she truly was. We came together as if a bulldozer had smashed away some of the emotional blocks within me. I knew that it was only me causing all the problems.

I was still unable to explain to her what had happened to me in my life before meeting her, but I was at least able to indicate that there was something wrong in my childhood, which made me frightened I would be a bad father. I promised that one day I would feel able to tell her everything. Not many people would have been understanding enough to be able to leave it at that. Most people would have demanded to know the whole story; would have felt that after such a betrayal they were owed a full explanation. Jackie was able to see that I wanted to be able to tell her about my demons, but for some reason wasn't able to. She worked as hard to convince me that I would be a great father as I was working to convince her that I loved her and wanted to have a family with her. Her kindness and understanding saved our relationship and retrieved my life from the total mess it could have descended into at that moment. The way she handled herself during those weeks and months made me admire and love her even more than I had before. We grew even closer and more in love. I found I was beginning to dwell less on my worries about how I would cope with the baby. The demons' voices seemed to be growing a little fainter in my head.

She came back home from her mother's and we started to prepare the house for the new arrival. The nursery looked fantastic, with Beatrix Potter pictures all over the walls. She had saved our relationship and our future and saved me from myself.

28

The Happy Ending

The first time Jackie had ever seen me cry was when I was standing beside her in the hospital with my daughter in my arms. I felt so happy. All my life I'd wanted to be someone else. Now I didn't want to be anyone other than myself. I had the most wonderful woman in the world and now I had this perfect baby daughter as well.

She was so tiny and soft, her face so purple after the efforts of nearly twenty-four hours of labour. My uncontrollable weeping was partly joy at holding my baby daughter in my arms, and partly relief because I realized that there was no way in the world I would ever be able to harm a hair on her head. Just as I had known when I met Jackie that I would never be able to hit her or abuse her in any way, I now knew that my daughter was going to be entirely safe in my care. I saw how foolish all my fears had been, how they had become exaggerated in my own mind, and I cried as if I would never stop, my shoulders heaving with the sobs, all inhibitions swept aside on a tide of emotion.

When we got home and started the business of looking after our precious new baby in earnest, I was desperate to do everything right. I wanted to be the exact opposite of my own parents. But as I cradled her in my arms, trying to soothe her to sleep, I realized I didn't know any nursery rhymes. So I made a point of sitting down and learning them. I wanted to be as close to the perfect father as I possibly could be. Despite the enormous effect music has had in my life, and despite the fact that I listen to it at every possible opportunity, I still sing very badly. But neither my daughter nor I cared about that. I just wanted to comfort her and she wanted to be comforted.

I was working hard selling in order to keep the money coming in and I hadn't forgotten my dreams of one day becoming a trader, but I kept having other ideas along the way. One time I put an advertisement into *Estates Gazette*, a British property magazine, asking for £250 million for a property portfolio I wanted to buy. I received between forty and fifty calls from people wanting to know more. Some of them were big companies, some small. I was still only twenty-four years old and I didn't have the knowledge or experience to convince any of them to take it any further, apart from one speculator who suggested we meet in London. He was exactly the sort of man I dreamed of becoming. He reminded me of who I wanted to be and what I should be focusing my energies on. He'd been down a couple of times but got back up and carried on fighting, which I admired more than anything – having the courage to get back up and fight when you're knocked down.

There was a big push on at work over a three-month period to meet the end of the year targets and we managed it, but then they didn't pay me for my extra efforts as agreed. To begin with I remained patient, because money was no longer as tight as it had been and I was not drowning in debt any more, but when I'd been asking them for the money for six months I decided I was being messed about, I'd given them enough chances to pay me. They didn't know about my past, although I had smacked a guy in the mouth for calling me an idiot when we were all out having a drink one night, so they should have guessed I wasn't willing to be jerked around for ever.

I was always in at work by seven in the morning and when the boss came in one morning I asked him where my money was, as I always did.

'Can I talk to you now?' I asked.

'Kevin,' he said, without breaking his stride, 'I'll talk to you about this later.'

It was a put-down and I was no longer willing to take it. I could see he was going to keep this up for ever if I didn't do something.

Once more I rang the friends who'd helped me in the past and two days later there were four guys parked outside the office in a car, waiting for me to call them in to sort things out. I was going to have to pay for their time, but it would be worth it if I got my money. I couldn't believe I still had to resort to these sorts of tactics, just because no one would pay me what they owed me. Yet again they would probably excuse themselves with, 'It's just business, nothing personal', but I was fed up with having to do this sort of business.

I walked into the boss's office.

'Morning, Kevin,' he said.

'I want to talk to you,' I said.

'Not now, Kevin,' he said, going back to his paperwork.

'If you don't talk to me now I've got four guys in a car outside who are going to come in and kick the shit out of you.' I gestured towards the window.

He looked puzzled for a moment, not sure if I was being serious or not. He stood up and walked to the window.

Looking out he saw the car and it was easy to see the sort of men who were sitting inside it.

'Why are you doing this?' he asked, in a voice that suggested I was betraying our friendship in some way.

'Because you're having a laugh at my expense,' I replied. 'All these months I've been grafting and you won't pay me what I'm owed.'

'What do you want me to do?' he asked.

'I just want you to pay me what you owe me from the end of the year when we made you all that money.'

Two hours later they gave me five grand and I was able to pay off the guys in the car.

'I don't think you can work for us any more,' the boss said when the business had been done.

'No,' I agreed, 'I don't think I can.'

'Hang on,' his partner interrupted. 'Let's talk about this.'

They knew I was hard-working and had made them money. After a few heated exchanges they offered me a new job.

'Listen,' I said. 'I'm going on holiday with Jackie. When I get back I'll let you know what I've decided.'

I'd never had a proper holiday in my life. Our little girl was eight months old and Jackie's mum was happy to look after her. We both needed a break. We headed down to the Maldives, which must be the most idyllic tropical paradise in the world. There were little wooden cottages on perfect white beaches, blue skies and blue waters; I'd never known peace like it. All my life I'd been dashing about, too hyper-active to be able to sit still for even a few minutes, but there I finally wound down and relaxed. I even read my first ever book (a John Grisham thriller). I was so chuffed with myself for having been able to read it all the way through. I spent hours every day just listening to music and clearing my mind. I felt I was finally ready to start my life properly, putting everything bad behind me. I told Jackie about my vision of becoming financially independent, and as I explained it to her in that perfect, peaceful setting, I realized I was now old enough and experienced and settled enough to start making my vision a reality. Sitting on that desert island, thousands of miles from home, I was able to see clearly that everything could now change – for the first time ever I felt completely relaxed and in love. Despite the perfection of the place we both missed our baby daughter dearly.

When we got back to England from the Maldives I started to study the financial markets and trading practices in earnest. I also read everything I could get hold of which would increase my knowledge on every front. I felt I had twenty-five years of catching up to do, from learning nursery rhymes for my daughter through to complex concepts of financial strategies. Something was still missing. My love for Jackie was the best thing that had ever happened to me. It gave me butterflies in my stomach every time I thought about her. I realized what was missing and proposed. Jackie accepted.

I was determined it would be a big romantic wedding, something that showed the world how much we loved each other and gave us all a day to remember. Jackie's family were all invited and had accepted, but there was a problem on my side. My invitation list included my friends, brothers and sisters, but not Gloria and Dennis. I was ashamed of my past and was nervous about inviting them. Naturally Jackie was curious as to why the invitation list didn't include my parents. She knew some things had gone on in the past, but not of anything that would stop my parents coming to our special day. At that time I didn't feel ready or able to tell her of my past, so it was easier for me to invite them. But also I wanted them to come to show the world I did have a family if only for a day. There was part of me that desperately wanted to have a normal family wedding.

I dreamed of having a perfect wedding day, with supportive parents who loved me, just like the weddings that occur every day all over the world. I dreamt my father was there for me giving me advice and support, and that my mother, future mother-in-law and Jackie would all get together and arrange and organize a magical day. Gloria and Dennis, as well as all my brothers and sisters were invited. Everyone except Robert, as nobody knew where he was. I knew Dennis would be too shy to be able to face such a crowd, but Gloria did come, together with my brother and sisters.

We held the reception in a marquee in the grounds of a beautiful old Georgian house. At the wedding Gloria was very quiet and throughout the day stayed close by her children – we rarely spoke. But what made my day, apart from Jackie and my little girl, was that my brother Wayne was by my side. We were true friends. My sisters seemed to enjoy the day too – for them it was an opportunity to escape their laborious life.

Three years after we had my daughter, my baby son came along. I couldn't believe my luck. I now had two perfect children. Holding a little replica of myself in my arms, I realized that I still had demons that needed to be brought out. But that was not the time. I was just too busy trying to secure our future to be able to spend time delving into emotional problems.

I went back to my old photocopying equipment company for a couple of months, just to show that I could, and then I left to set up on my own. I knew now I would never get together the money I needed working for other people. I had to have control of everything, which meant starting my own company.

The telephone and technology boom was in full swing and I decided I'd go into the business of setting up telephone systems for companies. I knew absolutely nothing about telephones, just as I'd known nothing about washing machines or photocopiers or the drinks businesses until I got into them, but I did know how to put in the hours and how to sell. I left my job one day and by the next I'd formed Synex Telecommunications Ltd for one pound and was on the phone selling to the companies that were already in my address book.

I began by just picking up the phone at home and making calls to see if I could find people who needed products. Most of the calls were fruitless, but I was starting to learn about the marketplace. I needed to get a dealership and I had a few thousand pounds saved. I went to see Ericsson to ask if I could represent their products. I could see they thought I was another dreamer who would give up as soon as he heard about the commitment they required for a dealership. They told me exactly what I'd need in the way of premises and trained staff before they would agree to me selling their products. They obviously didn't think they would ever be hearing from me again, but I now had something to aim at. Two months later I'd rented premises on the Purley Way in Croydon and I'd hired engineers. I also knew a few people who wanted to buy systems by then. Ericsson agreed to give me the dealership. Within three years Synex was employing over forty people and turning over just under £2.4 million.

As well as me working hard at the office, Jackie and I had also been doing up Margaret and Alan's old house, making it the best in the street, and eventually, when the property market had taken off again, we sold it for a nice profit and so were able to move, six or seven years after I'd bought it from Margaret. Although it was a beautiful house by the time we'd finished with it, I was keen to move away, to leave all the unhappy memories of my past behind and start somewhere completely fresh. I saw a tiny advertisement for a mock-Georgian house in the paper and went round to see it on my own. It'd been on the market for quite some time but hadn't sold. It was at the end of a cul-de-sac filled with the sort of perfect family homes you see in American movies, with white pillars round the doors and smooth green lawns sloping down to the road. In front of the house stood a forty-foot pine tree and that was what made my mind up. I could just picture how I would cover it with lights at Christmas-time. It would be like a fairy tale. I'd fallen completely in love with the place.

The house itself was in a pretty bad state, having been lived in by an old couple who hadn't done anything to it for years, but I could see through that to what it could be like. Jackie burst into tears when she saw how much work was going to be needed to get it up to the standard of our old house, but by then I was so bewitched by my vision of how it would look at Christmas she couldn't talk me out of it. It was the ideal family house and I worked on convincing her that we could turn it into a paradise.

The only thing I had going for me was my mouth, and I worked it morning, noon and night to bring in the business.

Any profits we made I invested back into the business and I kept a tight control of the finances. We were a professional company and a number of high-profile customers trusted us. I made sure I always paid everyone on time. I wanted to get a reputation for being someone who always kept his word. The industry was booming to such an extent there was room for everyone, and I was willing to work harder than anyone else to win the business and to serve clients to my utmost ability. We landed a number of big contracts from well-known companies. I had a team of sales people, but I was making the majority of the sales myself. It was hard work but I was proud of everything I was achieving. I set up another division in the company, which sold call time and line rental.

I had plans to expand across the country but it was hard to get staff because it was a boom time and bigger companies were offering salaries that we could never match. I came across a whole team of sales people who were willing to open up a Birmingham office for me. They were an experienced team from a rival who told me they would be bringing customers with them. I had no reason to disbelieve them and we opened a Birmingham office. The promised sales failed to materialize and our overheads soared. I'd made a fatal error. There was now friction between the London and Birmingham offices. I had been in discussion with a venture capital company about putting money in with the idea of floating it on the stock exchange. They were impressed with our track record but it didn't happen. The market was turning and the boom time was coming to an end. When I saw that we were getting into trouble I decided to take evasive action. I phoned up the chairman of a property company whose business we were tendering for and suggested that they buy us out. They provided serviced offices, with about seven thousand customers, and were planning to put our services into all of them. I was very honest and told him that I wanted to close the Birmingham office to cut my losses and then sell him the London operation.

We had a meeting and he agreed in principle to buy the company at a fair price, but told me to keep the Birmingham office open because their head office was up there. I was so happy. All my dreams were coming true. At last I was going to have the financial independence I'd always craved. I respected the company chairman and didn't feel we needed to employ expensive lawyers. Everything seemed to be working out well. Because Birmingham was still running the money was going out fast and the deal was taking several months to complete. I went to one last meeting to finalize everything and they told me they weren't going to buy the company. By that time I was in a fair amount of debt because I'd kept the Birmingham office open and had been supporting the sales team.

I didn't know what to say. I was now in serious trouble. No one else was going to buy the company now it was carrying so much debt. I'd put all my faith in them, been completely honest, and everything had collapsed.

'Do you want to buy any of the business?' I asked.

'We'll buy the call time and line rental part,' he replied and I realized that was all they had been after from the start. I told him I'd think about it.

On the way home I hit the wheel of my car on a kerb and ended up, stuck in the middle of nowhere, changing a tyre with all my dreams in tatters, when just a few hours before I'd believed I was a free man. To cap it all I couldn't even get the wheel off. I felt desolate.

I didn't sleep at all that night, just paced up and down trying to see a way out. In the end I had to do the deal they wanted. I was so angry with myself. I could see they'd played the game brilliantly, that it was not personal, that it was 'just business' and I had been naïve. I had to close down the rest of the company and call in the liquidators. I felt so bad about the people I was letting down.

In some ways I'd been a good employer, in others I know I wasn't. I was good at giving people a chance, especially people who hadn't been given a chance before, and it nearly always paid off. But I'm not a 'people person'. I suppose I had that beaten out of me at a very early age. If employees rang in sick or came to me with moans, which always seemed very petty to me, I'd have a lot of trouble empathizing with them. Overall I knew I'd be happier working on my own at my own pace, not having to worry about other people's needs or hurt feelings.

Although the eventual outcome of the deal was a fantastic disappointment, I had come out of it with a bit of money and for the first time in my life we had some to spare. We took the children to Disneyworld in Florida for my daughter's sixth birthday and it was as big a treat for me as it was for them. Even this tiny glimpse of one corner of America confirmed all my beliefs about what a wonderful country it was. Part of my payment had been in shares, which I'd been told I could sell at any time. I tried to sell them before we went to America but was told they hadn't been released to be sold. The price then collapsed. When I came back I decided to fight for compensation because I felt I'd been cheated. The stress of dealing with lawyers was enormous but I was determined not to give up. In the end I couldn't stand it any more. I bypassed the lawyers and went directly to the finance director of the company and laid my cards on the table. He convinced me that they hadn't done it on purpose but he did agree to make a settlement. It was a lot less than I'd been expecting when I started into the sale, but it was something, and at least it meant that I could move on and put the past behind me.

Selling the company meant that I finally had some time to sit back and think about where I had got to and what I still needed to do with my life. I'd found that having a son had brought many of the feelings about my own childhood I'd been suppressing for so long bubbling to the surface once more.

Although I had everything I wanted in life and was happier than I'd ever dreamed possible, I became upset because I could see myself as a small child when I looked at him. I realized how helpless and in need of protection I'd been and how badly I'd been betrayed by those who were meant to be looking after me. I'd managed to push my past into a box at the back of my mind and block it off, but now it was impossible not to be reminded of just how bad it had been. When I saw how little and vulnerable my son was, how dependent on us to guard him and look after him and guide him in the right directions, I realized all over again how much I'd missed. When I read about cases of child abuse and murder I understood how close I had come to being one of those children in the papers and it made me angry. I knew I needed to do something about dealing with the demons once and for all.

29

Looking Back Through Other Eyes

In 1993 a large envelope came through my door. It contained a green cardboard folder with a compliments slip from Social Services attached. There was no explanation as to what it was or why I'd been sent it. I glanced at it, but at that time I didn't want to be reminded of my past and it seemed to just contain information from files. It didn't interest me enough to go any further. I put it away, thinking I might look at it later, and then forgot about it.

Several years later I came across it again and looked more closely. I realized it was information the social workers had written after visiting my family. It had been prepared at the time they finally decided to find me a foster home and I was taken to Alan and Margaret. As I read I was transported back into the family house, suddenly seeing us all through someone else's eyes. The picture was horribly vivid and told me things about Gloria and Dennis I'd never known.

Gloria was born in 1941, so she was almost thirty by the time she had me. Dennis was two and a half years younger. At the age of five Dennis was sent to a children's home, his father having been killed in the war and his mother being unable to care for him. Having not seen her for three years, he moved back when an uncle came to live with her. When he was ten he was held responsible for setting fire to a haystack and went back to the children's home, where he remained until he was fourteen.

The social worker wrote that Dennis was of limited intelligence and suffered poor health, having had an operation for cancer of the testes and a vasectomy in 1977, which would explain why they never had any more kids after Brenda. The file explained that he was then diagnosed with epilepsy and retired from British Rail on medical grounds. Apparently, he also suffered from psoriasis when life became too stressful at home.

Then the report turned its attention to Gloria. Apparently she was the eldest of five children and experienced two long separations from her family during childhood and adolescence. She spent a year in hospital when she was eleven after being badly burned and at the age of seventeen was admitted to hospital again under Section 6 of the Mental Deficiency Act. That piece of information certainly made sense. All her behaviour became more understandable in the light of mental problems, if not forgivable. She remained in that hospital for about five years. In 1974, when I was three years old, she was put on probation for two years for defrauding the DHSS. That explained why she was never given a book for her Giro payments, why they always sent them through each week.

'To say the least,' a social worker had written, 'this is a chaotic family in every respect. The parents' limited intelligence and lack of understanding of, and inconsistency in, childcare has resulted in a very turbulent style of life. On a practical level, the family have consistently had problems in handling money and maintaining a clean and hygienic house. When they were living in New Addington their house used to smell of urine and the children had been observed urinating on the floor.

'In terms of management the family's record is poor. The parents' attempts at control have been inconsistent and sometimes out of proportion. Physical hitting has been perceived as the main method of controlling the children. All the children seem to be very active, boisterous, loud and attention seeking. It feels as if they're vying with each other for the parental affection that exists (and to some extent this affection is quite real). The situation has been exacerbated by the parents' tendency to make favourites of certain of the children and scapegoats of others.'

I paused for a moment to get my breath. Scapegoats were certainly what Robert and I had been. All the memories came flooding back. After a while I felt strong enough to continue reading.

'This picture of a noisy, chaotic family, limited parental coping abilities and material deprivation provides the context for numerous reports of suspected child abuse which this department has received since November '74, in respect of all the children, but in particular Kevin.'

So the reports were getting through. They did know what was going on. All the time that I was being beaten black and blue the Social Services knew about it. They knew that my life was in danger, but still they left me there.

The report talked of meetings that had been held and decisions taken to do nothing due to a lack of concrete evidence. It talked of places I was taken to before Yarborough that I don't remember, and of reports that one foster family sent me back because I was aggressive towards their other children, insolent and disobedient. When we moved from New Addington the social worker reported that he was going to try to make our family 'less dependent' on Social Services.

'This was not an easy task,' he reported, 'as Mrs Lewis made great efforts to pull me into the family life. She wanted to use me as a listening ear and was not pleased when it became clear I would not fulfil this function.'

If only there had been someone listening.

'Visiting the Lewis family is neither an easy or pleasant task as one is invariably beset by a scene of chaos. The noise level is quite unbearable as the members of the family communicate by screaming and shouting rather than by talking. Throughout interviews, the children make constant demands on Mrs Lewis' attentions – again in competition with each other. When they don't get the response they want they're very quick to kick up such a fuss that their demands cannot go unnoticed. Thus, it is absolutely imposs-ible to do "family" focused work with them.'

The report went on to describe how Gloria was the main spokesman and Dennis literally hung around in the background, sliding off to the kitchen if anything vaguely awkward was discussed.

'One gets the feeling with him that life and his family are all too much for him – I've never seen him smile; he always looks worn out, ill, harassed and is quick to anger. Mrs Lewis is a loud lady with whom it is very difficult to have a normal conversation in that it is virtually impossible to get her to focus on a specific issue that I might be there to discuss. As my contact has been less than that of her previous social worker, it feels that when I do see her she has to give me a complete run down on everything that's happened to her during the weeks since I'd last seen her.'

They then went on to talk about each of the children, admitting that Robert was one of the scapegoats.

'His school reported that he had a bruise under his eye. Robert said that his mother had hit him, his mother denied it. With no independent witnesses, the truth remains hidden – however, Mrs Lewis is known to lie.'

They confirmed that Brenda was Gloria's favourite and that Wayne was skipping school. It finally got round to me.

'Kevin now says, quite openly, that he has no feelings for his mother, that he hates her. My observations of their interactions suggest that there is little love lost between them and it is certainly fair to say that Kevin is not Mrs Lewis' favourite.

'When Kevin is shown affection he can be a lovely lad. He himself returns any affection shown to him and can be very loving. He can be polite and pleasant, thoughtful and eager to please. He has an uncanny, almost over-sophisticated, ability to analyse himself, his needs and his thoughts and verbalize his analysis. On the other side I have seen him purple with rage when in conflict with his mother. He is the recipient of quite severe physical punishment and has now learned to fight back.

'For whatever reasons, there is now little love between Kevin and his parents. Kevin comes across as a child starved of, and desperate for, some affection. He clings to people who show him some care (e.g. his Year Head at school). Kevin himself certainly contributes to the antagonism between himself and his parents, but this does not alter the facts that it is very likely that some of his basic needs are not being met.

'Kevin is at a point where the chaos is over-whelming

him and perhaps we need to offer a light at the end of the tunnel.'

I guess that is all that anyone can ask for, a light at the end of the tunnel.

30

Reflection

I had several reasons to write this book. I wanted to tell Jackie my story so she would understand why I am the way I am. I wanted to sort out the thoughts and feelings that watching my son grow up had brought out in me. And I wanted people to know what it is like for those who have nothing and no one when they start out in life, to maybe make them a little more tolerant and understanding of people who are different, and see what has gone into making them that way.

In some ways it was an easy story to tell because I'd lived it and remembered almost every stage with horrible clarity. Some of it I enjoyed writing, but other bits were painful to relive, reminding me of things I had carefully forgotten. The thought of trying to get the book published was even more frightening. I was worried that I was selling my soul and fretted at the thought of the questions that publishers and the public might ask once I'd submitted the manuscript to the world. I thought it would help me to exorcize my demons, and perhaps it will when it's all over, but it has also released others that I had been keeping carefully locked up.

When I look back at my life so far I can see how lucky I've been. Things could so easily have gone differently. When I hear on the news of children who have been abused and murdered I know exactly what they have been through.

I know what leads children to turn to crime and prostitution and how poverty destroys their lives and souls. I have escaped from that.

I've always wanted to do what's right and that has driven me on to the next thing each time as I've struggled to get as far away from my childhood as possible. Jackie changed everything for me and for that I owe her my heartfelt thanks. I also owe thanks to Uncle David and the staff at Yarborough for the comfort and security they offered me during my time there, and to Colin Smith whose persistence got me to Alan and Margaret's and introduced me to music. Then there was Gini who gave me respite during some of the most difficult times, Alan who sowed the seeds of ambition, and the friends who stayed with me through thick and thin. Then there are my children, who have brought me so much happiness in ways they will never understand.

I'm grateful to my brother, Wayne, for keeping in contact, and to all the people who don't know that they have helped me in some way, like you have by taking the time to read this book.

I have seen that what goes around comes around and now my parents are getting older and need love, comfort and support, but there is no one there for them. I could never bring myself to treat them as normal grandparents and take the children round for visits, and so they have to go on waiting.

They are both still living alone, deserted by their family and without friends. He spends most of his time in the pub; she sits in the house, desperate for company but unable to make a single friend. None of my brothers and sisters have managed to escape in the way I have. Robert is still with the funfairs, I believe. I hear about him now and then through the others. Wayne lived at home with Gloria until he was thirty, and now he's living with his girlfriend's parents. My three sisters have fifteen children between them. They all live in terrible flats in deprived areas, reliant on the state for every penny. They're trapped now until their children are old enough to stand on their own feet, but they won't have done anything by then, so who's going to employ them? I hope they don't fall even further through the net.

I still miss Alan, even after ten years. I feel my own life is finally beginning and I would have loved to share it with him. I haven't enjoyed it much up till now but at last I have a family to support who support me in return. My head is full of ideas of what I want to do next. Jackie and I have sold our dream house to give ourselves the capital we need to build the next stage of our lives. I don't know exactly what I will do yet, but for the first time ever I have choices. I've enjoyed writing and would like to continue to have the freedom to write. At present I'm writing my second book, this time a novel. I like inventing things, writing trading systems for the financial markets and looking for new opportunities. There are so many things to do that it's hard to choose. It was tough saying goodbye to the house that we all loved so much and which held so many happy memories, but we have to move on. I may not have had anyone to guide me in life at the beginning, but now I have my own experience to look back on and it tells me that you have to keep trying and that you can't stay still.

Today my passion is to learn. I spend hours lost in books, from studies of Leonardo da Vinci to some of the most complex equations the financial markets have to offer, from the stories of great explorers to woodworking and creative structures.

I'm no longer afraid of who I am. After wanting to be someone else for so long I'm finally glad to be me. Music has continued to be an enormously liberating influence and I now sing all the time, very badly I must confess, particularly when I'm alone in the car. It must look a strange sight to other drivers. My musical tastes vary from Rachmaninov to Missy Elliot, from Marilyn Manson to Elvis.

I still have dreams of what else I'd like to achieve. I'd like to have a house with a bit of land round it, so I could be at peace when I wanted to, and I'd like to travel all over America and Canada with Jackie. I'd like a little more financial security to remove the last few worries and I'd like to be able to ring the bell at the New York Stock Exchange; that has always symbolized freedom to me.

I sometimes go for long walks in the local countryside. The wide-open fields help me clear my head and think about the future – I rarely dwell on the past any more.

I know one day I'll have fields of my own and spend days smelling the sweet air and listening to the wind singing through crops I've planted myself. Now it seems as if anything is possible. If I lost it all tomorrow I'd get up the next day and start again because I've learnt that the most precious thing we possess is life itself.

These days I want to try everything that life has to offer. I can't resist any of the extreme sports; maybe I miss the adrenaline that I was brought up on. I also want to learn to paint and I tried learning the piano, but it made my knuckles ache from the damage that was done in the fights. I know my painting's not very good but with each new picture I find I can express myself more freely. I'm passionate about cooking and being able to use fresh produce is something I will never take for granted. I love taking the kids to school and working on ideas for new opportunities.

Today I'm so happy I can't stop bouncing from one thing to another. With all the stress of having to deal with other people gone, I don't even have problems with the bulimia any more. On family occasions like Christmas and birthdays I get even more excited than the children. They tell me Santa comes to the house every year, but I always seem to be out when he calls, or in the garage. The children's favourite time is when Mr Ticklehand comes out to play and the house erupts into laughter and screams of excitement and happiness. When they have birthday parties and all their friends bring them presents I have to hold tightly on to my emotions, in case my happiness for them and my memories of what birthdays can be like overflow. Sometimes, after we've switched the lights out at night, I turn my head away from Jackie so she won't see the tears in my eyes. But now they're tears of happiness.

I'm now going to sit down and raise a large glass of red wine to everyone who helped me through the first thirty years of my life. And to thank you for reading this book – you have made it all worthwhile. Now it's time to get on with fulfilling my dreams.